GOODSON MUMBA

Mastering Management Accounting

Strategies for Financial Excellence

Copyright © 2024 by Goodson Mumba

All rights reserved. No part of this publication may be reproduced, stored or transmitted in any form or by any means, electronic, mechanical, photocopying, recording, scanning, or otherwise without written permission from the publisher. It is illegal to copy this book, post it to a website, or distribute it by any other means without permission.

First edition

ISBN: 9798335506151

This book was professionally typeset on Reedsy.
Find out more at reedsy.com

Contents

Preface		iv
Acknowledgement		vi
Dedication		vii
Disclaimer		viii
1	Chapter 1: A New Challenge	1
2	Chapter 2: The Foundation of Change	19
3	Chapter 3: Budgeting for Success	29
4	Chapter 4: Implementing Advanced Costing Systems	41
5	Chapter 5: Performance Measurement Breakthroughs	57
6	Chapter 6: Strategic Management Accounting in Action	75
7	Chapter 7: Navigating Capital Budgeting Decisions	89
8	Chapter 8: Optimizing Working Capital	102
9	Chapter 9: Strengthening Internal Controls	115
10	Chapter 10: Decision-Making Excellence	129
11	Chapter 11: Cost Management Innovations	141
12	Chapter 12: Financial Planning and Analysis	154
13	Chapter 13: Leveraging Technology in Accounting	166
14	Chapter 14: Preparing for the Future	178
15	Chapter 15: Conclusion: Mastering Financial Excellence	191
About the Author		202

Preface

In today's dynamic business landscape, achieving financial excellence is no longer a mere aspiration but a critical necessity. As organizations strive to navigate the complexities of the global market, the role of management accounting has evolved from a traditional financial stewardship function to a pivotal driver of strategic decision-making and sustainable growth.

"Mastering Management Accounting: Strategies for Financial Excellence" is a comprehensive guide designed to equip professionals with the knowledge, tools, and insights required to excel in this transformative field. Whether you are a seasoned practitioner seeking to enhance your expertise or an emerging professional eager to make your mark, this book provides a roadmap to mastering the art and science of management accounting.

Each chapter delves into a critical aspect of management accounting, offering practical guidance, real-world examples, and actionable insights to help you navigate the complexities of financial management and drive excellence in your organization.

The journey begins with understanding the foundational elements of management accounting and progresses to advanced topics such as budgeting, cost management, performance measurement, and strategic planning. Along the way, you will encounter stories and case studies that bring these concepts to life, illustrating their application in real-world scenarios.

As you embark on this journey through the pages of "Mastering Management Accounting," I encourage you to approach each chapter with an open mind and a willingness to embrace new ideas and perspectives. The field of management accounting is ever-evolving, and staying ahead requires a commitment to continuous improvement, innovation, and strategic thinking.

Ultimately, this book is not just about mastering techniques and tools; it is about cultivating a mindset of excellence and a passion for driving positive change within your organization. It is about understanding the critical role that management accounting plays in achieving financial success and using that knowledge to make informed, strategic decisions that propel your organization forward.

Thank you for choosing to join me on this journey. I hope that "Mastering Management Accounting: Strategies for Financial Excellence" serves as a valuable resource and a source of inspiration as you navigate your path to financial excellence.

Sincerely,
Goodson Mumba

Acknowledgement

I would like to eternally and gratefully acknowledge the Almighty God for the infinite intelligence from His universal mind where we draw from all that we come to know and are yet to know. May I also acknowledge and thank everyone that has played a part in my journey of life in terms of spiritual, moral, emotional and material support.

Dedication

I extend my sincerest gratitude to my beloved wife, Edith Mumba, and our children, Angelina, Lubuto, Letticia, Lulumbi, and Butusho, for their unwavering support and understanding throughout the conception, writing, and eventual publication of this book, despite the sacrifices and challenges they endured.

Disclaimer

This book is a work of fiction. Names, characters, businesses, places, events, and incidents are either the products of the author's imagination or used in a fictitious manner. Any resemblance to actual persons, living or dead, or actual events is purely coincidental.

1

Chapter 1: A New Challenge

Introduction to Michael's Career and Current Role

Michael Anderson sat at his polished mahogany desk, staring at the quarterly reports sprawled out before him. The office was quiet except for the hum of computers and the occasional rustle of papers from the few employees working late. As the Senior Management Accountant for GlobalTech Industries, Michael had spent over a decade meticulously analyzing financial data, implementing cost-saving measures, and guiding the company's financial strategy. Yet tonight, he felt a gnawing sense of dissatisfaction.

His office, located on the fifteenth floor of the sleek corporate headquarters, overlooked the bustling cityscape. The view was a constant reminder of the heights he had reached in his career. From a fresh graduate with a degree in accounting, Michael had climbed the corporate ladder with precision and dedication, earning accolades and promotions along the way. His expertise in financial analysis and cost management had made him indispensable to GlobalTech.

Despite his success, Michael felt that something was missing. Each day had begun to blur into the next, the routine of meetings, report analysis, and budget reviews feeling increasingly monotonous. He had mastered the technical aspects of his job, but the thrill of new challenges seemed to have faded.

Just as he was contemplating his next steps, his phone buzzed, jolting him back to the present. It was an email from his boss, Rebecca Holt, the Chief Financial Officer of GlobalTech.

"Michael, urgent meeting tomorrow at 9 AM. Need your expertise on a critical issue. – Rebecca"

Michael's curiosity was piqued. Rebecca was not one to overstate matters; if she said it was critical, it truly was. He quickly typed a response confirming his attendance and leaned back in his chair, wondering what the issue could be.

The next morning, Michael arrived at the conference room to find Rebecca and several other senior executives already seated, their expressions grim. The air was thick with tension.

"Thank you for coming on such short notice," Rebecca began, her tone serious. "We've uncovered some financial discrepancies that could have significant implications for our year-end results."

Michael's heart raced. This was exactly the kind of challenge he had been longing for, albeit not in the way he had expected. He listened intently as Rebecca explained the situation. A recent internal audit had revealed discrepancies in cost allocations and budgeting errors that had gone unnoticed for months. The financial health of several key projects was at risk.

"We need to get to the bottom of this immediately," Rebecca continued. "Michael, I want you to lead a special task force to investigate and resolve these issues. Your expertise in cost management and your thorough approach make you the ideal person for this job."

Michael felt a surge of adrenaline. This was a chance to make a tangible impact, to utilize his skills in a way that mattered. "I'll get started right away," he replied, his voice steady with determination.

As the meeting adjourned, Michael felt a renewed sense of purpose. This was his opportunity to break free from the mundane routine and prove his worth in a new, challenging context. He returned to his office, his mind already racing with ideas and strategies to tackle the crisis.

Sitting back at his desk, Michael realized that this could be the turning point he needed. The path ahead was uncertain, but he was ready to face it head-on. He opened a fresh notebook and began to outline his plan, each stroke of the pen a step toward mastering not just management accounting, but his own career's potential for financial excellence.

Michael's Feeling of Professional Stagnation

As the sun began to set, casting a warm orange glow over the cityscape outside his office window, Michael leaned back in his chair, staring blankly at the ceiling. The day's meetings had provided a flurry of information and a renewed sense of purpose, yet underneath the surface, a familiar feeling of unease gnawed at him.

He swiveled his chair to face the window, the city lights flickering to life as the daylight faded. Michael had always found comfort in the hustle and bustle of the city below, but lately, the view felt more like a metaphor for his own life—

busy and vibrant on the outside, but with a creeping sense of emptiness within.

Michael had been with GlobalTech for over a decade, climbing the ranks from a junior accountant fresh out of college to a respected senior management accountant. His walls were adorned with framed certificates and awards, each a testament to his hard work and dedication. Yet, despite these accolades, he couldn't shake the feeling that he was simply going through the motions.

He remembered the early days of his career, filled with excitement and the thrill of new challenges. Every day had been an opportunity to learn, to grow, to prove himself. But now, the days felt monotonous. Meetings, reports, and numbers—always the same routine. The passion he once felt for his work seemed to have dwindled, replaced by a sense of stagnation.

Michael's phone buzzed, interrupting his thoughts. It was a text from his wife, Emily: "Don't forget, dinner with the Thompsons tonight at 7. See you soon! :)"

He glanced at the clock. It was already 6:15. With a sigh, he packed up his briefcase and headed out, trying to shake off the lingering melancholy. As he drove home, he reflected on his career path. He had achieved so much, yet the question loomed larger than ever: Was this all there was?

Arriving home, Michael was greeted by the cheerful chatter of his children and the comforting aroma of dinner cooking. Emily was bustling around the kitchen, setting the table and trying to keep the kids from causing too much chaos. She looked up and smiled as he walked in.

"Hey, how was your day?" she asked, her eyes filled with warmth and curiosity.

"It was…busy," Michael replied, forcing a smile. "A lot going

CHAPTER 1: A NEW CHALLENGE

on at work."

As they sat down to dinner with their friends, the conversation flowed easily, but Michael found his mind wandering. He listened with half an ear to the Thompsons' stories of their recent vacation, all the while grappling with the realization that he needed something more in his professional life.

Later that night, after the kids were tucked in bed and the house was quiet, Michael and Emily sat together in the living room. Emily, sensing his distraction, gently touched his arm.

"What's really going on, Michael?" she asked softly. "You've been distant lately."

He sighed, running a hand through his hair. "I don't know, Em. I just feel…stuck. I've been doing the same thing for years, and it feels like I'm not moving forward. Today's meetings were a reminder of how routine everything has become."

Emily nodded, her expression empathetic. "Maybe this new project will be the change you need. It sounds like a real challenge."

"Maybe," Michael agreed. "But I need to find a way to reignite that passion I used to have. I want to feel like I'm making a real difference, not just crunching numbers."

As he spoke, a sense of determination began to replace his earlier despondency. Emily's faith in him was unwavering, and her words gave him hope. He decided then and there that he would use this new challenge not just to help the company, but to rediscover his own drive and purpose.

The next morning, Michael arrived at the office early, a newfound resolve in his step. He was determined to tackle the project head-on, to dig deeper into the financial discrepancies, and to find innovative solutions that would not only resolve the issues but also reignite his passion for his work.

Sitting at his desk, Michael opened his notebook and reviewed his notes from the previous day's meetings. He began drafting a detailed action plan, outlining the steps he would take to understand the cost drivers and rectify the discrepancies. This was his opportunity to break free from the monotony and prove to himself that he still had the passion and the drive to excel.

With a clear sense of purpose, Michael dove into his work, ready to face the challenges ahead. This time, he was not just crunching numbers—he was on a mission to make a real difference, both for GlobalTech and for himself.

A Crisis Meeting at the Corporation Highlighting Financial Discrepancies

Michael had barely settled into his office when he received a message from Rebecca Holt, the CFO, summoning him to the executive conference room. The urgency in her tone was unmistakable. Grabbing his notebook and pen, Michael hurried down the hall, his mind racing with possibilities.

When he entered the room, the atmosphere was tense. Rebecca sat at the head of the table, her expression grim. Around the table were other key executives—David from Operations, Linda from HR, John from Production, and Samantha from Marketing. Each looked equally concerned, their faces etched with worry.

"Thank you for coming on such short notice," Rebecca began, not wasting any time. "We've uncovered some serious financial discrepancies during our latest internal audit. These issues could have significant implications for our year-end results and potentially our stock price."

CHAPTER 1: A NEW CHALLENGE

A murmur of concern rippled through the room. Michael could feel the weight of the situation pressing down on everyone. Rebecca continued, flipping through a stack of reports.

"It appears there are substantial variances in cost allocations and budgeting across several departments. If not addressed immediately, this could impact our financial stability and investor confidence."

Michael leaned forward, his professional instincts kicking in. "Can we get a detailed breakdown of where these discrepancies are most pronounced?" he asked.

Rebecca nodded, gesturing to a large screen at the front of the room. "I'll walk you through the key areas. Linda, could you start with the discrepancies in payroll and staffing?"

Linda cleared her throat, adjusting her glasses. "We've had unexpected increases in severance payouts and hiring costs. Several high-profile hires were not accounted for in the initial budget, leading to significant overspending in our HR department."

Rebecca then turned to John. "John, what about production?"

John looked visibly stressed. "Our primary supplier faced disruptions, forcing us to source materials at a higher cost. Additionally, we've been running significant overtime to meet project deadlines. These factors weren't anticipated in our budget forecasts."

Michael took diligent notes, his mind already forming a plan of action. As each department head detailed their issues, it became clear that the financial discrepancies were widespread and complex. Marketing's overspending on a major campaign and Operations' unexpected maintenance costs were also contributing to the problem.

Rebecca concluded the overview with a heavy sigh. "We need to address these issues immediately. Michael, given your expertise, I'd like you to lead a special task force to investigate and resolve these discrepancies. We need a clear, actionable plan to present to the board by the end of the week."

Michael felt a surge of determination. This was the kind of challenge he had been craving. "I'll start by meeting with each department head individually to understand the specifics. We need to identify the root causes and implement corrective measures as quickly as possible."

The meeting adjourned, and Michael lingered for a moment, gathering his thoughts. Rebecca approached him, her expression softening slightly.

"Michael, I know this is a lot to handle, but I have complete confidence in your abilities. We need your leadership now more than ever."

"Thank you, Rebecca," Michael replied. "I won't let you down."

Leaving the conference room, Michael felt a mix of urgency and excitement. The crisis had reignited his passion, providing him with a clear sense of purpose. He headed straight to his office, ready to roll up his sleeves and dive into the task ahead.

Back at his desk, Michael began by organizing a series of meetings with each department head. He knew that to solve this problem, he needed to understand every detail. As he mapped out his approach, he couldn't help but feel a renewed sense of vigor. This was his chance to not only resolve a critical issue but also to prove to himself that he was still capable of making a significant impact.

The task ahead was daunting, but Michael was ready. With a deep breath, he picked up the phone to schedule his first meeting, determined to get to the bottom of the financial discrepancies and steer GlobalTech back on track. This was more than just another project—it was an opportunity to reignite his passion and redefine his career.

Michael is Tasked with Leading a Special Project to Address These Issues

Michael walked briskly back to his office, the weight of the crisis meeting still heavy on his shoulders. The urgency and complexity of the situation were daunting, but he felt a spark of determination ignite within him. This was his chance to break free from the stagnation that had been plaguing him and to prove his worth in a high-stakes scenario.

His phone buzzed just as he reached his desk. It was a follow-up email from Rebecca, detailing his new responsibilities as the leader of the special project tasked with addressing the financial discrepancies. The email outlined immediate steps: gather a dedicated team, conduct a thorough analysis of the discrepancies, and develop a corrective action plan.

Michael took a deep breath, feeling the magnitude of the responsibility settling in. He started by calling his assistant, Karen, to help set up a war room—an operations hub where the team could work intensively over the next few weeks.

"Karen, I need you to book the large conference room for the next two weeks, starting tomorrow morning," Michael instructed. "Also, please send out invites for an initial task force meeting at 9 AM tomorrow. Make sure to include department heads from operations, production, marketing, and HR."

"Got it, Michael," Karen replied, sensing the urgency in his voice.

Next, Michael reviewed the list of potential team members who could bring diverse expertise to the project. He chose a mix of seasoned professionals and dynamic up-and-comers, aiming for a balance of experience and fresh perspectives. Once the invitations were sent, he turned his attention to preparing for the first meeting.

That evening, as Michael drove home, his mind was a whirlwind of strategies and potential solutions. He arrived to find Emily waiting for him with a warm smile and a comforting dinner. Sensing his preoccupation, she gave him space, knowing he needed to process the day's events.

"Thanks for understanding," he said, giving her a grateful kiss on the cheek. "It's a critical time at work, and I'll need to focus intensely for the next few weeks."

"We're here for you," Emily replied softly. "Just remember to take care of yourself too."

The next morning, Michael arrived at the office before dawn, armed with coffee and a stack of financial reports. He spent the early hours reviewing the data, looking for patterns and anomalies. By the time the task force gathered in the newly designated war room, he was ready.

The room buzzed with a mix of anticipation and anxiety as the team assembled. Michael stood at the front, projecting confidence despite the underlying tension.

"Thank you all for being here on such short notice," he began. "As you know, we've identified significant financial discrepancies that need immediate attention. Our goal is to understand these issues in detail, identify the root causes, and implement corrective actions swiftly."

He glanced around the room, meeting the eyes of each team member. "I've chosen this team because I believe each of you brings unique strengths to the table. We'll be working closely together over the next few weeks, and I need your full commitment and expertise."

Michael outlined the initial plan: daily briefings, detailed analysis sessions, and regular updates to senior management. He divided the team into subgroups, each tasked with focusing on specific areas such as cost allocation, budgeting errors, and unexpected expenses.

"Let's start by digging into the reports from each department," Michael directed. "We need to identify where the discrepancies are most pronounced and gather all relevant data."

As the team dispersed to their tasks, Michael felt a renewed sense of purpose. The war room became a hive of activity, with charts and spreadsheets covering the walls, and intense discussions filling the air. Michael moved between groups, offering guidance and absorbing their findings.

Over the next few days, the team uncovered a series of contributing factors: unanticipated supplier costs, overtime expenses, aggressive marketing campaigns, and staffing changes. Each discovery brought them closer to understanding the full picture, and Michael could see a path forward beginning to form.

One evening, as the team wrapped up another long day, Michael gathered everyone together. "We've made significant progress," he announced. "But there's still a lot of work to be done. I'm proud of the dedication and hard work each of you has shown. Together, we'll get through this and come out stronger on the other side."

Returning to his office, Michael felt a mix of exhaustion and exhilaration. Leading this special project was challenging every aspect of his expertise and pushing him to grow in new ways. The professional stagnation he had felt was being replaced by a sense of purpose and determination.

This crisis was not just a test of his skills, but a chance to reignite his passion for his work and to make a lasting impact on GlobalTech. As he looked out over the city lights once more, he felt a renewed confidence. He was ready to lead his team through this challenge and to emerge stronger than ever.

Introduction of Michael's Mentor, Sarah, Who Provides Guidance

It was late in the evening when Michael finally took a moment to stretch and glance at the clock. The war room had cleared out, and the building was eerily quiet. He was reviewing the day's findings when his phone buzzed with a text message. It was from Sarah Turner, his mentor and a retired CFO who had been a guiding force in his career since his early days at GlobalTech.

"Michael, heard about the crisis. Are you free for a call?"

Michael's eyes lit up. He hadn't spoken to Sarah in a few weeks, and her timing couldn't have been better. He quickly texted back, "Absolutely. Can we talk now?"

A few moments later, his phone rang. "Sarah, it's great to hear from you," he said, trying to mask the exhaustion in his voice.

"Michael, you sound tired. Tell me what's going on," Sarah's voice was warm and reassuring, a stark contrast to the turmoil he had been immersed in all day.

Michael sighed, running a hand through his hair. "It's been a rough few days, Sarah. We've uncovered significant financial

CHAPTER 1: A NEW CHALLENGE

discrepancies across multiple departments. Rebecca has tasked me with leading a special project to address the issues. It's a huge responsibility, and honestly, I'm feeling the pressure."

"I understand," Sarah replied thoughtfully. "I've been through similar situations. It's daunting, but it's also an opportunity for you to shine. Tell me more about what you've discovered."

Michael spent the next few minutes detailing the various issues—unexpected supplier costs, overtime expenses, marketing overspend, and staffing changes. Sarah listened intently, occasionally interjecting with probing questions.

"Michael, it sounds like you have a comprehensive understanding of the problems," Sarah said after he finished. "What you need now is a clear strategy to tackle them systematically. Let's break it down."

Sarah's calm, methodical approach was exactly what Michael needed. They began by identifying the most critical areas to address immediately. Sarah emphasized the importance of prioritizing actions based on their potential impact on the company's financial health.

"First, focus on the supplier costs and overtime expenses," Sarah advised. "These are likely the biggest contributors to your discrepancies. Can you negotiate better terms with your suppliers or find alternative sources? And for overtime, look into operational efficiencies that could reduce the need for extra hours."

Michael nodded, jotting down notes. "I'll start there. What about the marketing and staffing issues?"

"For marketing, you need to assess the ROI of the recent campaigns," Sarah continued. "If they're not delivering the expected returns, you'll have to make tough decisions about scaling back or reallocating resources. As for staffing, work closely with HR to review hiring practices and severance policies. Ensure that future hires are aligned with your budget forecasts."

Michael felt a surge of gratitude. Sarah's guidance was invaluable, cutting through the complexity with practical, actionable steps. "Thank you, Sarah. This helps a lot. I've been feeling overwhelmed, but breaking it down like this makes it more manageable."

"Remember, Michael, leadership isn't about doing everything yourself," Sarah added. "Leverage your team's strengths. Delegate tasks and empower them to take ownership of their areas. And don't forget to communicate regularly with Rebecca and the other executives. Keeping them informed will help maintain their confidence in your leadership."

As they wrapped up the call, Michael felt a renewed sense of clarity and determination. Sarah's words had not only provided a roadmap for addressing the financial discrepancies but had also reminded him of the importance of leadership and collaboration.

"Thanks again, Sarah. I don't know what I'd do without your guidance," Michael said sincerely.

"You're more than capable, Michael. Trust yourself and your team. You'll get through this," Sarah replied, her voice filled with confidence in him.

Michael hung up, feeling a weight lift off his shoulders. He quickly revised his action plan based on Sarah's advice, ready to present it to his team the next morning. As he locked up the war room for the night, he felt a spark of excitement. This challenge was his opportunity to grow, to lead, and to reignite his passion for his career.

CHAPTER 1: A NEW CHALLENGE

With Sarah's guidance in mind, Michael was ready to tackle the financial crisis head-on, confident that he could steer GlobalTech back on track and emerge stronger than ever.

The Decision to Re-evaluate the Company's Accounting Practices

Michael arrived at the office early the next morning, buoyed by his conversation with Sarah. The first rays of dawn filtered through the glass windows, casting a soft glow over the war room. He knew that today would be pivotal in their quest to address the financial discrepancies plaguing GlobalTech.

As his team trickled in, Michael called them to gather around the large conference table. His demeanor was calm but resolute, a reflection of the newfound clarity and determination he felt.

"Good morning, everyone," Michael began, looking each team member in the eye. "I want to start by saying how proud I am of the work we've done so far. We've identified several key areas that need our immediate attention. But to get to the root of these discrepancies, we need to take a step back and look at our accounting practices as a whole."

The room was silent, the weight of his words hanging in the air. Karen, his assistant, handed out the latest reports as Michael continued.

"I've been reviewing our processes, and it's become clear that part of the issue lies in how we track and allocate costs. If we're going to solve these problems and prevent them from happening in the future, we need to re-evaluate and possibly overhaul our accounting practices."

Linda from HR raised her hand. "Michael, are you suggesting

a complete audit of our current systems?"

"Yes," Michael replied. "A thorough audit and re-evaluation. This will be a significant undertaking, but it's necessary. Our current practices are leading to inefficiencies and inaccuracies that we can't afford to ignore."

John from Production spoke next. "I agree. The inconsistencies in our cost allocations have been a recurring issue. We need a more robust system."

Samantha from Marketing nodded in agreement. "And clearer guidelines on budgeting and ROI tracking would help us avoid overspending."

Michael felt a sense of validation. His team understood the gravity of the situation and the need for comprehensive change. He turned to Rebecca, who had joined the meeting to offer her support.

"Rebecca, can you share your perspective on this?" Michael asked.

Rebecca leaned forward, her expression serious. "Michael is right. We've been reactive for too long, putting out fires without addressing the underlying issues. A re-evaluation of our accounting practices will not only help us resolve these discrepancies but also position us for sustainable growth. I fully support this initiative."

Michael outlined the next steps. "We'll begin with an internal audit to identify specific weaknesses in our current systems. Karen, please coordinate with the finance team to gather all necessary documentation. Once we have a clear picture, we'll work with an external consulting firm to implement best practices and new technologies where needed."

He paused, gauging the team's reaction. There was a mix of apprehension and determination in their faces.

CHAPTER 1: A NEW CHALLENGE

"This will be a challenging process," Michael admitted. "But it's an opportunity for us to improve and innovate. We'll need to work closely together, support each other, and remain focused on our goal: to make GlobalTech's financial operations a benchmark for excellence."

The room was filled with a renewed sense of purpose. Michael's confidence was infectious, and his team was ready to tackle the challenge ahead.

After the meeting, Michael stayed back to finalize the details with Rebecca. "Thank you for backing me up," he said.

"You're doing great, Michael," Rebecca replied. "This is a critical moment for us, and your leadership is exactly what we need."

As Michael walked back to his office, he felt the weight of the responsibility but also the thrill of the challenge. This decision to re-evaluate the company's accounting practices was bold and necessary. It was a chance to fix what was broken and build something better, something resilient.

He spent the rest of the day coordinating the audit, meeting with department heads, and setting up a timeline for the re-evaluation process. Each conversation, each decision brought them closer to their goal.

That evening, as he left the office, Michael looked up at the GlobalTech building, its lights twinkling against the night sky. He felt a deep sense of accomplishment. The path ahead was still fraught with challenges, but for the first time in a long time, he felt truly engaged and purposeful.

Michael knew that the journey to re-evaluate and overhaul the company's accounting practices would be long and arduous. But with his team's support, Sarah's guidance, and his own renewed determination, he was ready to lead GlobalTech toward a future of financial excellence.

2

Chapter 2: The Foundation of Change

Michael Revisits the Basics of Cost Classification and Behavior

The war room hummed with activity as Michael gathered his team for the first session of their accounting practices re-evaluation. Charts and graphs covered the walls, a testament to the intensive analysis that had already begun. But before diving into the intricacies of GlobalTech's financial systems, Michael knew they needed to establish a solid foundation.

"Good morning, everyone," Michael began, his voice commanding attention. "Today, we're going back to basics. We need to ensure we have a clear understanding of cost classification and behavior before we can make any meaningful changes to our accounting practices."

He gestured to the whiteboard behind him, where he had already started sketching out diagrams of cost structures and behaviors. "Cost classification is the cornerstone of financial analysis. It allows us to categorize costs based on their nature and function, providing insights into how they affect our operations."

Karen, his assistant, handed out printed materials outlining the key concepts. Michael continued, his passion for the subject evident in every word. "There are several ways we can classify costs: by function, by behavior, by traceability, and by controllability. Today, we'll focus on cost behavior, as it's fundamental to understanding how costs change in relation to activity levels."

He pointed to a graph showing the relationship between total costs and production volume. "Costs can be classified as either variable or fixed based on how they respond to changes in activity. Variable costs fluctuate in direct proportion to changes in production or sales volume, while fixed costs remain constant regardless of activity levels."

Michael paused, allowing the information to sink in. He could see the gears turning in his team members' minds as they absorbed the concepts.

"Let's take an example," he said, turning to the whiteboard. "The cost of raw materials is typically a variable cost. As production increases, we need to purchase more materials, leading to higher costs. On the other hand, the cost of rent for our facilities is a fixed cost. It remains the same whether we produce 100 units or 1,000 units."

As the discussion unfolded, Michael encouraged his team to ask questions and engage in active dialogue. He knew that establishing a solid understanding of these basic principles was crucial to their success in overhauling GlobalTech's accounting practices.

"Now that we've reviewed the basics of cost classification

and behavior, we can apply this knowledge to our analysis of the financial discrepancies," Michael concluded. "Our goal is to identify areas where our current practices are falling short and develop solutions that will drive efficiency and accuracy in our financial operations."

The team nodded in agreement, their expressions focused and determined. Michael could sense their growing confidence as they delved deeper into the intricacies of cost analysis.

As the session came to a close, Michael felt a surge of pride. The foundation had been laid for meaningful change at GlobalTech. With a solid understanding of cost classification and behavior, his team was ready to tackle the challenges ahead and build a financial system that would propel the company toward a future of success.

Meeting with Department Heads to Understand Cost Drivers

Armed with a renewed understanding of cost classification and behavior, Michael wasted no time in putting theory into practice. He called for a meeting with the department heads to delve deeper into the specific cost drivers affecting each area of the business.

The conference room buzzed with anticipation as Michael welcomed the department heads, his demeanor confident and purposeful. He had prepared meticulously for this meeting, armed with charts, reports, and probing questions.

"Thank you all for being here," Michael began, projecting his voice to command attention. "As part of our efforts to re-evaluate GlobalTech's accounting practices, it's crucial that we understand the specific cost drivers within each department.

Our goal is to identify where costs are being incurred and how they impact our overall financial performance."

Karen, his assistant, handed out printouts of the latest financial reports as Michael launched into the discussion. "Let's start with operations. David, can you walk us through the primary cost drivers in your department?"

David, the head of operations, stood up, adjusting his glasses. "Certainly, Michael. Our biggest cost drivers are typically related to raw materials, labor, and overhead. With recent expansions, we've also seen an increase in equipment maintenance costs."

Michael nodded, scribbling notes furiously. "And have there been any changes in production processes or workflows that might be impacting these costs?"

David hesitated for a moment before responding. "Yes, we've implemented some new efficiency measures to increase output, but they've come with additional training and setup costs."

Next, Michael turned to Linda from HR. "Linda, how are staffing costs impacting our bottom line?"

Linda stood, her expression serious. "Staffing costs have been a significant challenge, especially with recent hires and terminations. We've also had to invest in training programs to upskill our workforce, which has added to our expenses."

Michael nodded thoughtfully, absorbing the information. "And Samantha, what about marketing? How are our campaigns affecting our financials?"

Samantha leaned forward, her eyes bright with enthusiasm. "Our marketing campaigns have been driving increased brand awareness and customer engagement, but they come with a hefty price tag. We've been investing heavily in digital advertising and promotional events to stay ahead of the competition."

As the meeting progressed, Michael drilled down into the specifics of each department's cost drivers, probing for insights and uncovering hidden inefficiencies. His team listened intently, offering their expertise and insights to the discussion.

By the end of the meeting, Michael had a comprehensive understanding of the key factors driving costs across GlobalTech. Armed with this knowledge, he was ready to develop targeted strategies to address the financial discrepancies and drive efficiency throughout the organization.

"Thank you all for your insights," Michael said, rising from his seat. "We have a lot of work ahead of us, but I'm confident that together, we can overcome these challenges and position GlobalTech for long-term success."

As the department heads filed out of the conference room, Michael felt a sense of accomplishment wash over him. The foundation had been laid for meaningful change, and he was ready to lead his team into a future of financial excellence.

Implementing Cost Allocation Methods

With a thorough understanding of the company's cost drivers and inefficiencies, Michael knew it was time to implement targeted cost allocation methods to address the financial discrepancies at GlobalTech.

Gathered once again in the war room, Michael stood at the front of the room, a whiteboard behind him filled with equations and diagrams. His team looked on attentively, ready to put their newfound knowledge into action.

"Alright, team," Michael began, his voice steady and determined. "Based on our analysis of the cost drivers, it's clear that we need a more accurate and transparent method of allocating costs across departments. Our current system is outdated and lacks granularity, leading to inefficiencies and inaccuracies in our financial reporting."

He turned to Karen, his assistant, who had been instrumental in compiling the data for their analysis. "Karen, can you walk us through the shortcomings of our current costing system?"

Karen nodded, standing to address the group. "Our current system relies primarily on broad, predetermined cost rates that are applied uniformly across departments. This one-size-fits-all approach fails to account for the unique activities and resource consumption patterns of each department, leading to misallocation of costs and distorted financial performance metrics."

Michael nodded, his mind already racing with ideas. "To address these shortcomings, we need to implement more sophisticated cost allocation methods that accurately reflect the utilization of resources by each department. This will require a detailed assessment of activity drivers and a shift towards activity-based costing."

He turned to his team, each member ready to play their part in this crucial undertaking. "We'll start by conducting an in-depth analysis of activity drivers within each department to identify the primary cost drivers. From there, we can develop cost pools and allocate costs based on the specific activities that drive resource consumption."

The team nodded in agreement, the gravity of the task ahead weighing heavily on their shoulders. But there was also a sense of determination, a shared commitment to implementing real change at GlobalTech.

Over the coming weeks, the team worked tirelessly to gather

data, analyze activity patterns, and develop a comprehensive cost allocation model. They collaborated closely with department heads, soliciting their input and expertise to ensure the accuracy and relevance of the new system.

As they neared completion of the project, Michael called for one final meeting to present their findings and recommendations to senior management.

"Thank you all for your hard work and dedication," Michael said, addressing the team gathered in the war room. "Implementing these cost allocation methods will not only address the financial discrepancies we've identified but also provide us with a more accurate and transparent view of our financial performance."

With a sense of pride and anticipation, the team finalized their presentation, ready to usher in a new era of financial excellence at GlobalTech. As they filed out of the war room, Michael couldn't help but feel a sense of optimism for the future. The foundation had been laid, and with their continued dedication and effort, he was confident that GlobalTech would emerge stronger than ever.

Training His Team on New Cost Classification Techniques

With the implementation of the new cost allocation methods underway, Michael recognized the importance of ensuring that his team was equipped with the necessary skills to navigate the changes effectively. Gathering them once again in the war room, he prepared to lead a comprehensive training session on the new cost classification techniques.

"Good morning, everyone," Michael greeted, projecting

an air of confidence and authority. "As we continue to overhaul GlobalTech's accounting practices, it's crucial that we all understand the intricacies of the new cost classification techniques we'll be implementing."

Karen, his trusted assistant, had prepared detailed training materials, which she distributed to each team member. Michael began the session by providing an overview of the rationale behind the shift to activity-based costing and the benefits it would bring to the organization.

"As we've discussed, our current costing system lacks granularity and accuracy," Michael explained, gesturing to the slides projected on the screen. "Activity-based costing allows us to allocate costs more precisely by directly linking them to the activities that drive resource consumption."

He proceeded to walk the team through the key concepts of activity-based costing, using real-world examples to illustrate its application in different departments of the company. His explanations were clear and concise, allowing even the most complex concepts to be easily understood.

"As part of this transition, each of you will play a vital role in implementing and maintaining the new cost allocation methods within your respective departments," Michael emphasized, his eyes scanning the room to ensure that his message resonated with each team member.

To reinforce their understanding, Michael organized interactive exercises and case studies, encouraging his team to apply the newly acquired knowledge to practical scenarios. He fielded questions with patience and insight, fostering an environment of open communication and collaboration.

As the training session drew to a close, Michael could sense a newfound confidence and enthusiasm among his team members. They were eager to put their training into practice and contribute to the success of the initiative.

"Thank you all for your participation," Michael said, concluding the session with a smile. "I have full confidence in each of you to embrace these new techniques and drive positive change within our organization. Together, we will pave the way for a future of financial excellence at GlobalTech."

As the team dispersed, Michael reflected on the productive session. He knew that training his team on the new cost classification techniques was a crucial step in ensuring the success of the initiative. With their knowledge and dedication, he was confident that they would rise to the challenge and help propel GlobalTech toward a brighter, more prosperous future.

Immediate Improvements Seen in Cost Reporting

In the days following the implementation of the new cost allocation methods, Michael and his team worked tirelessly to ensure a smooth transition. As the weeks passed, they monitored the impact of the changes closely, eager to see the results of their efforts.

One morning, as Michael settled into his office, he was greeted by an email from Rebecca with the subject line: "Cost Reporting Update." With a sense of anticipation, he opened the message to find a detailed report outlining the latest financial data.

As he scrolled through the report, Michael's eyes widened in disbelief. The numbers told a story of immediate improvements in cost reporting across the board. The discrepancies that had once plagued GlobalTech's financial statements were now significantly reduced, thanks to the more accurate and transparent cost allocation methods.

Excitedly, Michael called for a meeting with his team to share the news. As they gathered in the war room, he projected the updated cost reports onto the screen, highlighting the improvements that had been achieved.

"Team, I have some incredible news to share," Michael began, his voice filled with pride. "Thanks to your hard work and dedication, we've already begun to see tangible improvements in our cost reporting."

He pointed to the graphs and charts displayed on the screen, illustrating the reduction in variances and the increased accuracy of the financial data. His team members exchanged looks of satisfaction, their efforts validated by the positive results.

"This is just the beginning," Michael continued, his excitement growing. "With our new cost allocation methods in place, we have the foundation we need to drive even greater efficiency and accuracy in our financial operations."

As the meeting concluded, Michael couldn't help but feel a sense of triumph. The immediate improvements seen in cost reporting were a testament to the effectiveness of their efforts. With continued dedication and teamwork, he was confident that GlobalTech would continue to thrive and prosper in the days to come.

3

Chapter 3: Budgeting for Success

Overhauling the Corporation's Outdated Budgeting Process

With the foundation of change firmly established, Michael turned his attention to the next critical aspect of financial management: budgeting. The outdated budgeting process at GlobalTech had long been a source of frustration, hindering the company's ability to plan effectively for the future. Determined to usher in a new era of financial foresight and accountability, Michael set out to overhaul the corporation's budgeting process.

Gathering his team in the war room once again, Michael wasted no time in laying out his vision for the future. Charts and graphs adorned the walls, a visual representation of the data-driven approach he planned to implement.

"Good morning, everyone," Michael greeted, his voice brimming with enthusiasm. "As we continue our journey towards financial excellence, it's clear that we need to revamp our budgeting process from the ground up. The current system is antiquated and fails to provide us with the agility and accuracy we need to thrive in today's fast-paced business environment."

Karen, his ever-efficient assistant, distributed copies of the current budgeting guidelines, highlighting their shortcomings. Michael paced the room, his mind already racing with ideas for improvement.

"Our goal is to develop a budgeting process that is dynamic, collaborative, and aligned with our strategic objectives," Michael explained, his words echoing with determination. "We need a system that empowers department heads to take ownership of their budgets while providing senior management with the visibility and control they need to make informed decisions."

He outlined his plan to introduce rolling forecasts, allowing for real-time adjustments based on changing market conditions and business priorities. He also proposed implementing a zero-based budgeting approach, forcing each department to justify every expense from scratch, rather than simply adjusting previous budgets.

"As part of this overhaul, we'll also invest in new budgeting software to streamline the process and improve accuracy," Michael announced, his eyes alight with excitement. "This will enable us to consolidate financial data from across the organization, providing us with a single source of truth for decision-making."

The team nodded in agreement, energized by Michael's vision for the future. They understood the importance of modernizing the budgeting process and were eager to play their part in driving the transformation.

Over the coming weeks, Michael and his team worked

tirelessly to implement the changes outlined in his plan. They conducted training sessions to familiarize staff with the new budgeting software and provided ongoing support to ensure a smooth transition.

As the dust settled and the new budgeting process took shape, Michael couldn't help but feel a sense of pride. The corporation's outdated budgeting process had been replaced with a dynamic, forward-thinking approach that would position GlobalTech for success in the years to come. With their newfound agility and precision, they were ready to tackle whatever challenges lay ahead and chart a course towards financial prosperity.

Introducing New Budgeting Techniques, Including Zero-Based Budgeting

With the overhaul of GlobalTech's outdated budgeting process underway, Michael knew that introducing new techniques was essential to ensure the company's financial success. Among these techniques, zero-based budgeting stood out as a powerful tool to drive accountability and efficiency throughout the organization.

Gathering his team once again in the war room, Michael began the session with a sense of purpose and determination. Charts and diagrams adorned the walls, illustrating the principles of zero-based budgeting and its potential impact on the company's financial health.

"Good morning, everyone," Michael greeted, his voice infused with energy. "As part of our efforts to modernize our budgeting process, I'm excited to introduce you to a powerful tool: zero-based budgeting."

He explained the concept in detail, emphasizing its departure from traditional budgeting methods. "In zero-based budgeting, departments are required to justify every expense from scratch, rather than simply adjusting previous budgets. This forces us to reevaluate our spending priorities and allocate resources based on their strategic value to the organization."

Karen distributed copies of the new budgeting guidelines, outlining the steps required to implement zero-based budgeting within each department. Michael encouraged his team to embrace the challenge and approach it as an opportunity for innovation and improvement.

"We'll start by conducting thorough reviews of each department's activities and expenses," Michael explained, pacing the room with purpose. "This will allow us to identify areas of inefficiency and reallocate resources to where they can have the greatest impact."

The team listened intently, their expressions a mix of curiosity and determination. They understood the significance of this shift in approach and were eager to rise to the challenge.

As the meeting progressed, Michael led his team through practical exercises to familiarize them with the zero-based budgeting process. They analyzed case studies, identified cost-saving opportunities, and developed action plans to implement the new budgeting techniques within their departments.

By the end of the session, Michael could sense a palpable shift in the room. The team was energized by the possibilities offered by zero-based budgeting and eager to put their newfound knowledge into practice.

"As we embark on this journey together, remember that change won't happen overnight," Michael reminded them, his voice filled with conviction. "But with dedication, collaboration, and a commitment to excellence, I have no doubt that we will achieve our goal of financial success for GlobalTech."

With a renewed sense of purpose, the team dispersed, ready to embrace the challenges and opportunities that lay ahead. Armed with the principles of zero-based budgeting, they were poised to usher in a new era of financial accountability and efficiency at GlobalTech.

Engaging with Various Departments to Create Realistic Budgets

With the introduction of new budgeting techniques, including zero-based budgeting, Michael understood the importance of engaging with various departments to create realistic budgets that aligned with GlobalTech's strategic objectives. Armed with enthusiasm and determination, he embarked on a series of meetings with department heads to foster collaboration and transparency in the budgeting process.

In the bustling conference room, Michael sat at the head of the table, flanked by department heads representing every facet of GlobalTech's operations. Charts and graphs adorned the walls, providing a visual representation of the company's financial landscape.

"Thank you all for joining me today," Michael began, his tone both warm and authoritative. "As we work to create budgets that reflect our strategic priorities, it's essential that we collaborate closely to ensure alignment and accuracy."

He turned to the department heads, each one eager to contribute to the discussion. "I encourage you to approach this process with an open mind and a willingness to challenge assumptions," Michael continued. "Our goal is to develop budgets that are not only realistic but also forward-thinking, enabling us to seize opportunities and overcome challenges in the year ahead."

Over the course of the meeting, Michael led his team through a detailed review of each department's activities, expenses, and revenue projections. He encouraged open dialogue and debate, soliciting input from department heads to ensure that every aspect of the budget was thoroughly scrutinized and optimized.

"As we move forward, I urge you to prioritize investments that will drive long-term value for the company," Michael emphasized, his eyes meeting those of each department head in turn. "We must be strategic in our allocation of resources, focusing on initiatives that will fuel growth and innovation."

As the meeting drew to a close, Michael thanked his team for their contributions and commitment to the budgeting process. "I have full confidence in our ability to create budgets that will set us up for success in the year ahead," he said, his voice filled with optimism.

With a renewed sense of purpose, the department heads left the conference room, energized by the collaborative spirit and determined to create budgets that would propel GlobalTech toward a future of financial prosperity. As they returned to their respective departments, they knew that their efforts would play a vital role in shaping the company's success in the months and years to come.

Dealing with Resistance from Long-time Employees

Despite Michael's best efforts to foster collaboration and transparency, he encountered resistance from some long-time employees who were skeptical of the new budgeting techniques. As he navigated this challenge, Michael relied on his leadership skills to address their concerns and build consensus within the organization.

In a tense meeting with the finance team, Michael found himself facing a group of long-time employees who were wary of the changes he was implementing. The atmosphere in the room was palpably tense, with murmurs of discontent echoing off the walls.

"I understand that these changes may feel overwhelming," Michael began, his voice steady and measured. "But I assure you, they are necessary to ensure our long-term success."

One of the senior finance managers spoke up, his tone skeptical. "We've been using the same budgeting process for years, Michael. Why fix something that isn't broken?"

Michael met the man's gaze, his expression unwavering. "The world is changing, and so must we. Our current budgeting process is outdated and no longer serves the needs of our dynamic business environment. We need to embrace new techniques if we're going to stay competitive."

As the discussion continued, Michael listened attentively to the concerns raised by the finance team. He acknowledged their apprehension and took the time to address each point with patience and empathy. He emphasized the benefits of the new budgeting techniques, highlighting how they would provide greater visibility and control over the company's finances.

"It's natural to feel resistant to change," Michael said, his voice soft but firm. "But I believe that together, we can overcome these challenges and emerge stronger than ever. We owe it to ourselves and to GlobalTech to embrace innovation and drive positive change."

As the meeting concluded, Michael could sense a shift in the room. Though not everyone was fully convinced, there was a newfound sense of openness and willingness to explore the possibilities offered by the new budgeting techniques.

Over the following weeks, Michael continued to engage with the finance team, addressing their concerns and providing support as they navigated the transition. Through his unwavering leadership and commitment to collaboration, he was able to gradually build consensus and rally the team behind the vision for a more dynamic and effective budgeting process.

As resistance gave way to acceptance, Michael knew that the path to financial success for GlobalTech was within reach. With his team united and focused on a common goal, he was confident that they would overcome any obstacles and emerge stronger than ever.

Using Variance Analysis to Track Budget Performance

As the new budgeting process took root at GlobalTech, Michael turned his attention to implementing robust mechanisms for tracking budget performance. Variance analysis emerged as a key tool to monitor financial progress and identify areas for improvement, allowing Michael and his team to make data-driven decisions to steer the company towards its financial goals.

Gathering his team in the war room once again, Michael

began the session with a sense of purpose and urgency. Charts and graphs adorned the walls, displaying the latest budget figures alongside actual performance data.

"Good morning, everyone," Michael greeted, his voice commanding attention. "As part of our commitment to financial excellence, it's crucial that we track our budget performance closely to ensure we stay on course."

He outlined the principles of variance analysis, explaining how it compared actual financial results to budgeted expectations to identify discrepancies and their underlying causes. "By understanding these variances, we can take corrective action where needed and capitalize on opportunities for improvement," Michael explained, his words resonating with conviction.

Karen distributed copies of the latest variance reports, detailing deviations between budgeted and actual figures for each department. Michael encouraged his team to scrutinize the data and identify trends or anomalies that required further investigation.

"As we review these reports, I want each of you to consider what factors may have contributed to the variances we're seeing," Michael instructed, his gaze sweeping across the room. "Was it due to changes in market conditions, operational inefficiencies, or unforeseen events? By digging deeper into the root causes, we can gain valuable insights to inform our decision-making."

The team dove into the reports with fervor, analyzing the numbers and discussing potential explanations for the variances they observed. Michael facilitated the discussion, guiding his team to explore different perspectives and consider alternative hypotheses.

As the meeting progressed, a pattern began to emerge. Certain departments were consistently underperforming against their budgeted targets, while others were exceeding expectations. Through careful analysis and discussion, the team identified areas for improvement and developed action plans to address the underlying issues.

"As we move forward, I want each of you to take ownership of your department's performance and actively seek opportunities to drive efficiency and profitability," Michael urged, his voice filled with determination. "Variance analysis is not just about identifying problems—it's about empowering us to take proactive measures to achieve our financial goals."

With a renewed sense of purpose, the team dispersed, armed with the insights gleaned from the variance analysis. As they returned to their respective departments, they knew that their collective efforts would play a crucial role in shaping GlobalTech's financial trajectory. With variance analysis as their compass, they were ready to navigate the complexities of the business landscape and chart a course towards sustained success.

Michael's Personal Reflections on Managing Change

Alone in his office after a long day of meetings and strategizing, Michael took a moment to reflect on the whirlwind of change he had initiated at GlobalTech. As he gazed out of the window at the city skyline bathed in the warm glow of the setting sun, he couldn't help but feel a mixture of pride and apprehension.

The weight of responsibility hung heavy on his shoulders as he contemplated the journey ahead. Managing change was no easy feat, and Michael knew that the road ahead would be fraught with challenges and obstacles. Yet, he also harbored a deep sense of optimism and determination.

With a sigh, Michael leaned back in his chair, his thoughts drifting to the conversations and meetings that had filled his day. He recalled the resistance he had encountered from some long-time employees, the skepticism in their voices echoing in his mind.

But amidst the challenges, there had also been moments of triumph—small victories that reaffirmed his belief in the power of positive change. The immediate improvements seen in cost reporting, the enthusiasm of his team as they embraced new budgeting techniques, the sense of camaraderie forged through collaboration—each moment served as a reminder of the potential for transformation.

As he reflected on these experiences, Michael realized that managing change was as much about leading with empathy and resilience as it was about implementing new processes and techniques. It required patience, understanding, and a willingness to listen—to truly listen—to the concerns and perspectives of others.

With a renewed sense of purpose, Michael resolved to approach the challenges ahead with an open heart and an open mind. He knew that the road to financial excellence would be long and arduous, but he was ready to face it head-on, armed with determination and a steadfast belief in the power of change.

As the sun dipped below the horizon, casting a warm glow over the city, Michael felt a sense of peace wash over him. The journey ahead would be daunting, but he was not alone. With his team by his side and a clear vision guiding his steps, he was ready to navigate the twists and turns of the road ahead and lead GlobalTech towards a future of success.

4

Chapter 4: Implementing Advanced Costing Systems

Evaluating Different Costing Systems: Job Order, Process, and ABC

The war room hummed with anticipation as Michael gathered his team to embark on the next phase of their journey towards financial excellence: implementing advanced costing systems at GlobalTech. Charts and diagrams adorned the walls, a visual representation of the various costing methods they would evaluate.

"Good morning, everyone," Michael greeted, his voice resonating with energy and purpose. "Today, we're diving into the world of advanced costing systems—specifically, job order costing, process costing, and activity-based costing (ABC)."

He turned to the whiteboard, where he had already sketched out the key characteristics of each costing system. "Each of these methods offers unique advantages and challenges, and it's crucial that we carefully evaluate them to determine which one is best suited to our needs."

Karen, his trusted assistant, distributed handouts outlining the fundamentals of each costing system. Michael began by explaining job order costing, emphasizing its suitability for businesses that produce custom or unique products, such as custom-built machinery or specialized software.

"Job order costing allows us to track the costs associated with each specific job or project," Michael explained, his words punctuated by illustrations on the whiteboard. "This method provides a detailed breakdown of costs, making it ideal for businesses with diverse product lines or complex production processes."

Next, Michael delved into process costing, highlighting its applicability to industries with standardized, repetitive production processes, such as food manufacturing or chemical processing. "Process costing aggregates costs by department or process, providing a high-level view of production costs over time," he explained, drawing parallels between the method and GlobalTech's own manufacturing operations.

Finally, Michael turned his attention to activity-based costing (ABC), a more sophisticated costing method that allocates costs based on the activities that drive them. "ABC offers a more accurate and granular view of costs, allowing us to better understand the cost drivers within our organization," he said, outlining its potential to uncover hidden inefficiencies and inform strategic decision-making.

As the discussion unfolded, Michael encouraged his team to ask questions and engage in debate. He knew that selecting the right costing system would be critical to their success in optimizing costs and improving profitability at GlobalTech.

"Each costing system has its strengths and limitations,"

Michael concluded, surveying the room with a sense of satisfaction. "Our task now is to carefully evaluate each option and determine which one will best serve the needs of our organization."

With a renewed sense of purpose, the team set to work, diving into the details of each costing system and analyzing their applicability to GlobalTech's unique business operations. As they pored over data and debated the merits of each method, Michael couldn't help but feel a sense of excitement for the possibilities that lay ahead. With the right costing system in place, they would be one step closer to achieving their goal of financial excellence at GlobalTech.

Deciding on Activity-Based Costing for the Corporation

After days of intensive analysis and spirited debate, the team reconvened in the war room to make the pivotal decision that would shape the future of GlobalTech's financial management. Michael stood at the head of the table, his expression one of calm determination. The walls were covered with charts, graphs, and summaries of their findings on job order costing, process costing, and activity-based costing (ABC).

"Thank you all for your hard work and dedication over the past few days," Michael began, his voice resonating with a sense of purpose. "Today, we're here to decide which costing system will best meet our needs and propel GlobalTech towards financial excellence."

Karen handed out a final comparative analysis, summarizing the strengths and weaknesses of each costing method. Michael paused, giving everyone a moment to review the document before continuing.

"After careful consideration, it's clear that each system has its merits," Michael said, his eyes scanning the room. "Job order costing offers detailed tracking for custom jobs, and process costing is ideal for standardized production. However, the most comprehensive and adaptable system for our diverse and dynamic operations is activity-based costing."

A murmur of agreement rippled through the room, but Michael knew there were still reservations to address. He turned to Raj, the head of manufacturing, who had been one of the most vocal skeptics of ABC.

"Raj, I understand you have concerns about the complexity of implementing ABC," Michael acknowledged, his tone respectful yet firm. "But let's consider the long-term benefits. ABC will allow us to pinpoint the true cost drivers within our operations, leading to more informed decisions and greater efficiency."

Raj nodded slowly, his expression thoughtful. "You're right, Michael. It will be a challenge, but the potential for better cost management and improved profitability is undeniable."

Encouraged by Raj's openness, Michael continued. "ABC will enable us to allocate costs more accurately based on the activities that consume resources. This granularity will help us identify inefficiencies, streamline processes, and ultimately drive down costs."

He turned to Rebecca, the head of marketing, who had championed the idea of ABC from the start. "Rebecca, could you share your perspective on how ABC will benefit our marketing efforts?"

Rebecca leaned forward, her enthusiasm evident. "Absolutely. With ABC, we can better understand the costs associated with each marketing campaign and channel. This insight will allow us to allocate our budget more effectively and maximize our return on investment."

As the discussion continued, Michael could see the growing consensus among his team. The initial skepticism was giving way to a shared recognition of the potential benefits of ABC.

"Implementing ABC will require a concerted effort from all of us," Michael concluded, his voice filled with conviction. "But I have no doubt that together, we can make this transition successfully. By adopting ABC, we'll gain the insights we need to drive efficiency, optimize costs, and achieve our strategic goals."

With a unanimous nod of agreement, the decision was made. GlobalTech would adopt activity-based costing as its new costing system. As the team dispersed to begin the implementation process, Michael felt a surge of pride and optimism. The path ahead would be challenging, but with ABC as their guide, they were well-equipped to navigate the complexities of their business environment and steer GlobalTech towards a future of financial excellence.

Training Sessions with Team Members on ABC

The decision to implement activity-based costing (ABC) at GlobalTech had been made, and Michael knew that the next crucial step was ensuring that his team was well-equipped to navigate the new system. He organized a series of training sessions designed to demystify ABC and empower his team with the knowledge and skills they needed to excel.

In the company's largest conference room, rows of chairs faced a large screen displaying the agenda for the day's training session. Michael stood at the front, ready to kick off the first of many intensive workshops on ABC. His team filtered in, some excited, others apprehensive, but all eager to understand the new system that would revolutionize their operations.

"Good morning, everyone," Michael began, his voice carrying a mix of enthusiasm and reassurance. "Today marks the beginning of an important journey for GlobalTech. Implementing ABC is a significant change, but it's one that will bring us closer to our goal of financial excellence."

He started with the basics, explaining the principles of ABC, how it differed from traditional costing methods, and why it was the best fit for their organization. "ABC allows us to assign costs more accurately by linking them to specific activities. This will give us deeper insights into what drives our costs and how we can manage them more effectively."

As he spoke, Michael could see the initial trepidation in some of his team members' faces beginning to fade. He moved on to practical examples, using case studies from other companies that had successfully implemented ABC. "Let's look at how Company X improved their cost management and operational efficiency with ABC," he said, pointing to a detailed case study on the screen.

He then introduced Raj, the head of manufacturing, who had initially been skeptical but now stood as an advocate for ABC. "Raj will walk us through how we can apply ABC to our manufacturing processes. Raj?"

Raj stepped forward, his demeanor confident. "Thanks, Michael. At first, I was concerned about the complexity of ABC, but I've come to see its potential. By accurately tracing costs to specific activities, we can uncover inefficiencies we never knew existed."

Using diagrams and real-world scenarios, Raj explained

CHAPTER 4: IMPLEMENTING ADVANCED COSTING SYSTEMS

how ABC would be applied in the manufacturing department, breaking down complex concepts into understandable terms. The team asked questions, and Raj, along with Michael, provided clear, detailed answers.

Next, Rebecca from marketing took the floor. "In marketing, understanding our cost drivers is crucial. ABC will help us allocate our budget more effectively and ensure that every dollar spent contributes to our strategic goals," she explained, showing how ABC would bring precision to their campaign planning and execution.

The training sessions continued throughout the week, each one delving deeper into the specific applications of ABC across different departments. Hands-on activities, group discussions, and interactive exercises helped solidify the team's understanding. Michael made sure that each session was not only informative but also engaging, creating a supportive environment where team members felt comfortable asking questions and expressing concerns.

By the end of the week, the transformation was palpable. The initial apprehension had given way to a sense of empowerment and readiness. Michael addressed the team one last time. "I'm incredibly proud of the progress we've made this week. Implementing ABC is a collective effort, and your dedication and enthusiasm have been inspiring. Together, we're paving the way for a brighter, more efficient future for GlobalTech."

As the team filed out of the conference room, energized and equipped with the knowledge to tackle the challenges ahead, Michael felt a deep sense of accomplishment. They were ready to implement ABC, and with their newfound expertise, they were poised to lead GlobalTech to new heights of financial excellence.

Early Challenges and Troubleshooting During Implementation

The initial enthusiasm for the new activity-based costing (ABC) system quickly met the reality of implementation. Despite thorough training and preparation, Michael and his team encountered a series of early challenges that tested their resolve and ingenuity.

It was a gray Monday morning when the first signs of trouble emerged. Michael sat at his desk, sipping his coffee and reviewing the latest data integration reports. Karen rushed in, her face etched with concern.

"Michael, we've hit a snag," she said, handing him a stack of printouts. "The data from the manufacturing department isn't aligning with the ABC model. There are discrepancies in the cost allocations."

Michael frowned, scanning the reports. "Okay, let's gather the team and address this head-on. We knew there would be bumps along the way."

In the war room, Michael convened a meeting with key department heads, including Raj from manufacturing, Rebecca from marketing, and several IT specialists. The atmosphere was tense, but Michael's calm demeanor helped keep the focus on finding solutions.

"Alright, let's walk through the issues," Michael began. "Raj, can you explain what's happening with the manufacturing data?"

Raj nodded, his brow furrowed. "The problem seems to be with how we're tracking certain indirect costs. The system isn't capturing them correctly, and it's throwing off the entire allocation process."

CHAPTER 4: IMPLEMENTING ADVANCED COSTING SYSTEMS

Michael turned to the IT team. "Can we identify where the breakdown is happening in the data integration?"

One of the IT specialists, Linda, spoke up. "We believe it's an issue with the way the data is being formatted and uploaded. There might be inconsistencies in how different departments are reporting their activities."

"Alright," Michael said, thinking quickly. "Let's set up a task force to standardize the data reporting formats. Linda, work with Raj's team to ensure we're capturing the correct information."

Over the next few days, the task force worked tirelessly to troubleshoot the data issues. They identified several areas where data entry practices differed between departments, leading to inconsistencies. Standardizing these practices required patience and meticulous attention to detail, but gradually, they began to see improvements.

However, the challenges didn't stop there. Rebecca reported issues in marketing, where the ABC system was revealing unexpected cost drivers that her team was struggling to interpret.

"Michael, we're seeing costs allocated to activities that don't seem to make sense," Rebecca explained during a late-night call. "It's causing confusion and frustration among the team."

Michael listened carefully, then suggested, "Let's have a workshop to go over these findings. We need to understand why these costs are appearing and how we can address them. It's a learning process for all of us."

In the workshop, Michael and Rebecca worked through the data with the marketing team, identifying misclassified activities and clarifying the logic behind ABC allocations. The hands-on approach helped demystify the process, turning confusion into clarity.

As the weeks passed, more challenges emerged. Some team members felt overwhelmed by the increased workload and the steep learning curve. Michael made it a point to check in regularly, offering support and encouragement.

During one such check-in, he sat with Karen in the break room, both of them nursing cups of coffee. "It's been a rough start," Karen admitted, looking exhausted. "But I think we're getting the hang of it."

Michael smiled, nodding. "Implementing change is always hard, but we're making progress. We just need to keep pushing through and supporting each other."

Slowly but surely, the team began to see the fruits of their labor. The data discrepancies were resolved, and the standardized reporting processes took hold. The initial resistance gave way to a growing confidence in the ABC system.

One Friday afternoon, as Michael reviewed the latest reports, he felt a sense of accomplishment. The numbers were starting to align, and the insights generated by the ABC system were already helping to identify cost-saving opportunities.

He called a meeting to share the positive developments with the team. "I know it's been a challenging journey," he said, addressing the group. "But your hard work is paying off. We're starting to see the benefits of ABC, and it's only going to get better from here."

As he looked around the room, Michael saw the nods of agreement and the renewed determination in his team's faces. They had weathered the early storms, and together, they were forging a path toward financial excellence at GlobalTech.

Case Study: Success Story from a Department Using ABC

The initial challenges of implementing activity-based costing (ABC) at GlobalTech had been met with resilience and teamwork. Now, as the system began to take hold, success stories started to emerge, validating Michael's vision and the team's hard work. One such story came from the manufacturing department, where ABC had made a significant impact.

It was a bright Wednesday morning when Michael decided to share this success with the entire company. He gathered everyone in the large conference room, a sense of anticipation buzzing through the air. On the screen behind him was a presentation titled "ABC in Action: Manufacturing Department's Success."

"Good morning, everyone," Michael began, his voice filled with pride and excitement. "Today, I'm thrilled to share a success story from our very own manufacturing department. This case study highlights how ABC has transformed their operations and set a benchmark for the rest of us."

Raj, the head of manufacturing, took the stage next, his demeanor confident and enthusiastic. "When we first started with ABC, we faced numerous challenges," he admitted. "But thanks to the dedication and hard work of my team, we've seen incredible results."

Raj clicked to the first slide, showing a graph of the department's costs before and after ABC implementation. "These are our cost figures from six months ago compared to now. As you can see, there's a significant reduction in our overhead costs."

He went on to explain how ABC had helped them identify

and eliminate inefficiencies. "We discovered that a substantial portion of our costs were tied to unproductive activities. For example, we found that a lot of time and resources were being wasted on excessive machine setups and unnecessary quality inspections."

Using ABC, Raj's team mapped out each activity in their production process and linked costs directly to those activities. This granular insight allowed them to streamline operations, focusing on high-value tasks and reducing waste. "We implemented just-in-time production techniques and enhanced our quality control processes, cutting down on rework and improving overall efficiency," Raj explained.

The next slide showed a bar chart with the productivity metrics. "Not only did we reduce costs, but we also increased our production output by 15%," Raj continued. "This improvement has had a direct positive impact on our bottom line."

To illustrate the human side of this transformation, Raj introduced Carla, a production supervisor who had been instrumental in the change. Carla stepped forward, a mix of pride and humility in her expression.

"When ABC was first introduced, I was skeptical," Carla admitted. "It seemed like just another management fad. But as we started using it, I saw how it could genuinely help us. By understanding exactly where our time and money were going, we could make smarter decisions and improve our workflow."

Carla shared a specific example. "One of the biggest changes was in how we handled machine maintenance. Before ABC, we treated all maintenance the same, leading to frequent but unnecessary servicing. Now, we schedule maintenance based on actual usage and wear, which has reduced downtime and saved costs."

The audience listened intently, inspired by the tangible results and the real-world application of ABC. Michael could see the shift in their attitudes, from skepticism to belief in the power of the new system.

Raj concluded the presentation with a call to action. "Our success with ABC is just the beginning. I encourage all departments to fully embrace this system and look for similar opportunities to improve. The benefits we've seen are proof that with the right approach, we can achieve incredible things."

Michael stepped back to the podium, his heart swelling with pride. "Thank you, Raj and Carla, for sharing your story. This is exactly the kind of success we envisioned when we decided to implement ABC. Let's use this as a model and continue pushing towards our goal of financial excellence."

The room erupted in applause, a shared sense of accomplishment and motivation filling the space. As the meeting concluded, Michael felt a renewed sense of optimism. The success of the manufacturing department was a beacon of what was possible, and he was confident that, with continued effort and commitment, GlobalTech would achieve its ambitious goals.

Michael's Growing Confidence in His Leadership Abilities

The success story from the manufacturing department had rejuvenated the entire team at GlobalTech. As they dispersed from the conference room, buzzing with excitement and newfound motivation, Michael lingered a moment, soaking in the palpable sense of progress and possibility.

That evening, Michael found himself alone in his office,

reflecting on the journey thus far. He leaned back in his chair, staring at the city lights twinkling through the large windows. The road to implementing activity-based costing (ABC) had been fraught with challenges, but the triumphs were beginning to shine through, validating his decisions and reinforcing his leadership.

Michael's thoughts drifted back to the initial days of skepticism and resistance. He remembered the daunting task of convincing his team of the merits of ABC, the intense training sessions, and the troubleshooting that had tested their patience and resilience. Each hurdle had seemed insurmountable at the time, but together, they had overcome them, one by one.

A soft knock on the door interrupted his thoughts. Sarah, his mentor, stepped in, a warm smile on her face. "You did good today, Michael," she said, her voice filled with pride.

Michael smiled back, gesturing for her to take a seat. "Thanks, Sarah. I feel like we've finally turned a corner. Seeing the manufacturing department's success has been incredibly rewarding."

Sarah nodded, her eyes reflecting a mix of wisdom and encouragement. "Leadership is about more than just making decisions, Michael. It's about inspiring others to believe in those decisions and guiding them through the challenges. You've done that brilliantly."

Michael felt a surge of gratitude. "I couldn't have done it without your guidance. You've always known when to push me and when to offer support."

Sarah laughed softly. "That's what mentors are for. But today, it's clear you're coming into your own as a leader. You're no longer just implementing a new system; you're transforming this company and, in the process, yourself."

They talked for a while longer, reflecting on the journey and the lessons learned. After Sarah left, Michael sat quietly, feeling a profound sense of growth. He realized that his confidence in his leadership abilities had grown with each challenge they faced and each victory they achieved.

The next morning, Michael arrived at the office with a renewed sense of purpose. He walked the halls with a confident stride, stopping to chat with team members, offering words of encouragement, and answering questions about the ABC system. His presence was reassuring, a steady hand guiding the ship.

Later that day, Michael called another meeting with his core team. "We've seen the incredible potential of ABC in manufacturing," he began, his voice strong and steady. "Now, it's time to replicate that success across every department."

He laid out a strategic plan for the next phase of implementation, assigning key responsibilities and setting ambitious but achievable goals. The team listened intently, their trust in Michael's leadership evident in their focused expressions and eager nods.

Rebecca spoke up, her voice filled with enthusiasm. "With your guidance, Michael, I believe we can achieve even greater success. The manufacturing department's story has inspired us all."

Raj added, "We're ready to take on the next challenges, thanks to your leadership and vision."

Michael's heart swelled with pride. "Thank you, everyone. Our journey isn't over, but together, we're capable of amazing things. Let's continue to push boundaries and strive for excellence."

As the meeting adjourned, Michael felt a deep sense of

fulfillment. His confidence in his leadership abilities had been hard-earned through experience, perseverance, and the unwavering support of his team. With each step forward, he was not only transforming GlobalTech but also himself, emerging as a leader ready to guide his company to new heights.

5

Chapter 5: Performance Measurement Breakthroughs

Identifying Key Performance Indicators for Different Departments

The implementation of the ABC system at GlobalTech had set a strong foundation, and Michael was determined to build upon this momentum by focusing on performance measurement. He knew that identifying the right key performance indicators (KPIs) for each department was crucial for driving continuous improvement and achieving financial excellence.

One crisp morning, Michael convened a meeting with the heads of all departments. The atmosphere in the room was a mix of anticipation and determination, as everyone understood the importance of this next step in their transformation journey.

"Good morning, everyone," Michael began, his voice steady and confident. "Today, we're going to tackle the next critical phase of our initiative: identifying key performance indicators for each department. KPIs will help us measure our progress and ensure we're aligned with our strategic goals."

He turned to Karen, the CFO, who had been instrumental in the ABC implementation. "Karen, can you kick us off by explaining the importance of KPIs and how they will integrate with our new costing system?"

Karen nodded and stood up, her presence commanding yet approachable. "KPIs are essential metrics that provide us with insights into how well we are achieving our objectives. They are not just numbers; they tell a story about our operational efficiency, financial health, and strategic alignment. With the ABC system in place, we now have a more accurate way to track these metrics and make informed decisions."

Michael then divided the room into smaller breakout groups, each tasked with brainstorming potential KPIs for their respective departments. The energy in the room was palpable as department heads engaged in animated discussions, drawing on their deep understanding of their areas to identify the most relevant metrics.

Raj, leading the manufacturing group, spoke passionately about the need for precise operational KPIs. "We should track metrics like cycle time, defect rates, and equipment utilization. These will help us ensure that we're maximizing efficiency and maintaining high-quality standards."

Rebecca, heading the marketing group, emphasized the importance of customer-centric KPIs. "We need to focus on metrics such as customer acquisition cost, conversion rates, and customer lifetime value. These will give us a clear picture of our marketing effectiveness and how well we're engaging with our customers."

CHAPTER 5: PERFORMANCE MEASUREMENT BREAKTHROUGHS

In the IT breakout group, Linda highlighted the critical KPIs for technology infrastructure. "System uptime, incident response time, and user satisfaction scores are key. These will help us monitor our IT performance and ensure that we're providing reliable and efficient support to the entire company."

Michael moved between the groups, listening, providing input, and encouraging collaboration. He was impressed by the depth of insight and the level of engagement from his team. It was clear that they were not just going through the motions; they were deeply invested in this process and understood its importance.

After the breakout sessions, everyone reconvened in the main conference room to share their proposed KPIs. Each group presented their ideas, with Michael and Karen facilitating the discussions to refine and prioritize the metrics.

"Great work, everyone," Michael said, as the final list of KPIs was displayed on the screen. "We've identified the key metrics that will guide our performance measurement across all departments. Now, let's discuss how we will implement and track these KPIs to ensure they drive the right behaviors and outcomes."

Karen outlined the next steps, including integrating the KPIs into the company's reporting systems and establishing a regular review process. "We'll set up dashboards to provide real-time visibility into these metrics, and we'll hold monthly review meetings to assess our progress and make any necessary adjustments."

As the meeting wrapped up, Michael felt a sense of accomplishment and anticipation. Identifying and implementing KPIs was a significant milestone, but he knew it was just the beginning. The true test would be in how they used these metrics to drive continuous improvement and achieve their strategic goals.

He addressed the team one last time. "I'm incredibly proud of the work we've done today. Identifying these KPIs is a major step forward, but our success will depend on how effectively we use them to guide our actions and decisions. Let's stay focused and committed to our goals. Together, we can achieve financial excellence and set a new standard for GlobalTech."

The room erupted in applause, and as Michael looked around, he saw a team ready to embrace the challenges ahead with confidence and determination. They were on the brink of a performance measurement breakthrough, and with their newfound clarity and focus, there was no limit to what they could achieve.

Setting Up a Balanced Scorecard System

With the key performance indicators (KPIs) identified, Michael recognized the need for a comprehensive framework to align these metrics with GlobalTech's strategic objectives. A balanced scorecard system would provide the structure they needed to ensure that performance measurement was integrated across all levels of the organization.

On a sunny afternoon, Michael gathered his leadership team in the boardroom, the air humming with anticipation. The windows framed a breathtaking view of the city skyline, a reminder of the heights they aimed to reach.

"Good afternoon, everyone," Michael began, his voice carrying the weight of purpose. "Today, we're taking a significant step forward in our journey towards financial excellence. We're going to set up a balanced scorecard system to align our key performance indicators with our strategic goals."

He turned to Karen, who had been instrumental in designing the ABC system and was now tasked with spearheading the balanced scorecard initiative. "Karen, could you walk us through the concept of a balanced scorecard and how it will benefit GlobalTech?"

Karen stood, her expression determined. "A balanced scorecard is a strategic management tool that translates an organization's mission and vision into tangible objectives and metrics across four key perspectives: financial, customer, internal processes, and learning and growth. By balancing these perspectives, we ensure that our performance measurement is holistic and aligned with our long-term success."

She proceeded to outline each perspective, illustrating how they would map GlobalTech's strategic objectives to specific KPIs. "For example, under the financial perspective, we'll track metrics such as revenue growth, profit margins, and return on investment. These indicators will help us gauge our financial health and the value we deliver to our stakeholders."

Raj, Rebecca, and Linda nodded in agreement, recognizing the relevance of these perspectives to their respective departments. Michael could see the wheels turning in their minds, envisioning how their own KPIs would fit into this framework.

"We'll need input from each of you to ensure that the balanced scorecard reflects the unique priorities and challenges of your departments," Michael emphasized, his gaze sweeping across the room. "This is a collaborative effort, and it's essential that we align our objectives with the overall strategic direction of the company."

Over the next few weeks, Karen led a series of workshops to develop the balanced scorecard in collaboration with department heads. Together, they mapped out strategic objectives, identified KPIs for each perspective, and defined targets for performance improvement.

In the finance department, they focused on optimizing working capital and reducing overhead costs. In marketing, they aimed to enhance customer satisfaction and brand loyalty. In IT, they prioritized system reliability and innovation.

As the balanced scorecard took shape, Michael could sense a newfound sense of alignment and purpose among his team. Each department was now fully engaged in driving towards common goals, and the balanced scorecard provided the framework to ensure that their efforts were coordinated and focused.

Finally, on a crisp morning, Michael convened a meeting to unveil the completed balanced scorecard. The room buzzed with anticipation as Karen displayed the colorful diagram on the screen, each perspective adorned with its corresponding objectives and KPIs.

"This balanced scorecard represents our collective vision for the future of GlobalTech," Michael declared, his voice ringing with pride. "It's a roadmap that will guide our actions and decisions, ensuring that we stay true to our mission and achieve our strategic objectives."

As the team absorbed the details of the balanced scorecard, a sense of unity and purpose filled the room. They knew that this framework would not only drive performance improvement but also foster a culture of accountability and collaboration.

With the balanced scorecard in place, GlobalTech was poised to achieve new levels of success. As Michael looked around the room at his team, he felt a deep sense of gratitude and optimism. They had overcome countless challenges together,

Incorporating Financial and Non-Financial Performance Measures

With the balanced scorecard framework established, Michael recognized the importance of integrating both financial and non-financial performance measures to provide a comprehensive view of GlobalTech's performance. This holistic approach would enable them to make more informed decisions and drive continuous improvement across all aspects of the organization.

One brisk morning, Michael gathered his leadership team in the boardroom once again, the air tinged with anticipation. The windows offered a glimpse of the bustling city below, a reminder of the dynamic environment in which they operated.

"Good morning, everyone," Michael greeted, his voice filled with purpose. "Today, we're taking another significant step forward in our journey towards financial excellence. We're going to discuss how we can incorporate both financial and non-financial performance measures into our balanced scorecard framework."

He turned to Karen, who had been leading the charge on this initiative. "Karen, could you share why it's important for us to consider both financial and non-financial measures?"

Karen stood, her presence commanding yet approachable. "Financial measures provide us with valuable insights into our bottom line and financial health. However, they only tell part of the story. Non-financial measures, such as customer satisfaction, employee engagement, and innovation, are equally important in assessing our overall performance and long-term success."

She proceeded to outline how they would integrate these measures into the balanced scorecard, ensuring a balanced approach that captured both quantitative and qualitative aspects of performance. "By incorporating non-financial measures, we can better understand the drivers of financial performance and identify areas for improvement that may not be immediately apparent from financial data alone."

Raj, Rebecca, and Linda nodded in agreement, recognizing the value of this approach in their respective departments. Michael could see the enthusiasm in their eyes, eager to embrace this new dimension of performance measurement.

"We'll need input from each of you to ensure that we identify the most relevant non-financial measures for your departments," Michael emphasized, his gaze sweeping across the room. "This is an opportunity to capture the full spectrum of our performance and drive meaningful change across the organization."

Over the following weeks, Karen led a series of workshops to identify and prioritize non-financial measures in collaboration with department heads. Together, they brainstormed ideas, evaluated their relevance, and selected the most impactful measures for inclusion in the balanced scorecard.

In the marketing department, they focused on metrics such as customer satisfaction scores, brand perception, and market share. In IT, they prioritized measures related to system uptime, user satisfaction, and innovation initiatives. In manufacturing, they looked at metrics such as product quality, employee safety, and production efficiency.

As the discussions unfolded, Michael could sense a palpable energy in the room. The team was fully engaged in this pro-

CHAPTER 5: PERFORMANCE MEASUREMENT BREAKTHROUGHS

cess, recognizing the importance of capturing both financial and non-financial aspects of performance to drive holistic improvement.

Finally, on a bright afternoon, Michael convened a meeting to unveil the completed balanced scorecard, now enriched with both financial and non-financial measures. The room buzzed with anticipation as Karen displayed the updated diagram on the screen, each perspective adorned with a mix of quantitative and qualitative indicators.

"This balanced scorecard represents a comprehensive view of our performance as an organization," Michael declared, his voice filled with pride. "It's a testament to our commitment to excellence and our recognition that true success extends beyond the bottom line."

As the team absorbed the details of the balanced scorecard, a sense of unity and purpose filled the room once again. They knew that this holistic approach to performance measurement would enable them to drive meaningful change and achieve their strategic objectives in a way that honored their values and vision for the future.

With the balanced scorecard enriched with both financial and non-financial measures, GlobalTech was poised to embark on the next phase of its journey towards financial excellence. As Michael looked around the room at his team, he felt a deep sense of pride and gratitude. They had embraced this new dimension of performance measurement with enthusiasm and dedication, and together, they were ready to chart a course towards a brighter future.

Benchmarking Against Industry Standards

As GlobalTech continued its quest for financial excellence, Michael recognized the importance of benchmarking their performance against industry standards. Benchmarking would provide valuable insights into their relative performance, identify areas for improvement, and help them stay competitive in a rapidly evolving market.

On a crisp morning, Michael gathered his leadership team once again in the boardroom, the air filled with anticipation. The windows offered a panoramic view of the city skyline, a reminder of the dynamic landscape in which they operated.

"Good morning, everyone," Michael greeted, his voice filled with purpose. "Today, we're taking yet another step forward in our journey towards financial excellence. We're going to discuss how we can benchmark our performance against industry standards to gain insights and drive continuous improvement."

He turned to Karen, who had been leading the charge on this initiative. "Karen, could you share why it's important for us to benchmark our performance against industry standards?"

Karen stood, her demeanor poised and confident. "Benchmarking allows us to compare our performance metrics against those of our peers in the industry. By doing so, we can identify best practices, set realistic performance targets, and uncover opportunities for improvement. It's a crucial tool for staying ahead of the curve and maintaining our competitive edge."

She proceeded to outline their approach to benchmarking, which would involve gathering data on key performance indicators from industry reports, trade associations, and peer companies. "We'll analyze this data to assess our relative performance and identify areas where we excel and areas where we have room for improvement."

Raj, Rebecca, and Linda nodded in agreement, recognizing the value of this approach in their respective departments. Michael could see the determination in their eyes, eager to leverage benchmarking as a strategic tool for driving performance improvement.

"We'll need input from each of you to ensure that we select the most relevant benchmarks for your departments," Michael emphasized, his gaze sweeping across the room. "This is an opportunity to gain valuable insights and learn from the best in the industry."

Over the following weeks, Karen led a series of workshops to identify and prioritize benchmarks in collaboration with department heads. Together, they analyzed industry reports, studied peer companies, and evaluated their own performance against established standards.

In the marketing department, they benchmarked metrics such as customer acquisition costs, conversion rates, and brand awareness against industry averages. In IT, they compared metrics related to system uptime, response times, and cybersecurity measures. In manufacturing, they assessed metrics such as production efficiency, defect rates, and employee safety records.

As the discussions unfolded, Michael could sense a palpable sense of urgency in the room. The team recognized the importance of benchmarking as a strategic tool for driving performance improvement and were fully committed to leveraging this approach to stay ahead of the competition.

Finally, on a bright afternoon, Michael convened a meeting

to review the results of their benchmarking efforts. The room buzzed with anticipation as Karen presented the findings on the screen, comparing GlobalTech's performance against industry averages and highlighting areas of strength and areas for improvement.

"This benchmarking exercise provides valuable insights into our performance relative to industry standards," Michael declared, his voice filled with pride. "It's a roadmap for continuous improvement and a testament to our commitment to excellence."

As the team absorbed the details of the benchmarking analysis, a sense of determination filled the room once again. They knew that this information would empower them to make informed decisions, set realistic performance targets, and drive meaningful change across the organization.

With the benchmarking results in hand, GlobalTech was poised to embark on the next phase of its journey towards financial excellence. As Michael looked around the room at his team, he felt a deep sense of gratitude and optimism. They had embraced benchmarking as a strategic tool for driving performance improvement with enthusiasm and dedication, and together, they were ready to chart a course towards a brighter future.

Developing Performance Dashboards for Real-Time Tracking

With benchmarking insights in hand, Michael knew the importance of real-time tracking to ensure GlobalTech stayed on course towards financial excellence. Developing performance dashboards would provide the team with immediate visibility into key metrics, allowing them to make informed decisions and take timely corrective actions.

On a sunny morning, Michael gathered his leadership team once again in the boardroom, the atmosphere charged with anticipation. The windows offered a sweeping view of the cityscape, a reminder of the dynamic environment in which they operated.

"Good morning, everyone," Michael greeted, his voice filled with determination. "Today, we're continuing our journey towards financial excellence by developing performance dashboards for real-time tracking. These dashboards will provide us with immediate visibility into our key metrics, empowering us to make informed decisions and drive continuous improvement."

He turned to Karen, who had been leading the charge on this initiative. "Karen, could you share why it's important for us to develop performance dashboards?"

Karen stood, her demeanor poised and confident. "Performance dashboards provide us with a centralized platform to track our key performance indicators in real-time. They allow us to monitor our progress, identify trends, and take timely actions to address any deviations from our targets. It's a critical tool for fostering accountability and driving performance improvement across the organization."

She proceeded to outline their approach to developing the dashboards, which would involve leveraging data visualization tools to create dynamic and interactive displays of key metrics. "We'll design these dashboards to provide a comprehensive view of our performance across all departments, allowing us to quickly identify areas of strength and areas for improvement."

Raj, Rebecca, and Linda nodded in agreement, recognizing the value of this approach in their respective departments. Michael could see the excitement in their eyes, eager to leverage performance dashboards as a strategic tool for driving continuous improvement.

"We'll need input from each of you to ensure that we capture the most relevant metrics for your departments," Michael emphasized, his gaze sweeping across the room. "This is an opportunity to empower our teams with the information they need to succeed and to foster a culture of transparency and accountability."

Over the following weeks, Karen led a series of workshops to design and develop the performance dashboards in collaboration with department heads. Together, they identified the most critical metrics, designed visually engaging displays, and tested the functionality to ensure a seamless user experience.

In the marketing department, they focused on metrics such as website traffic, lead generation, and campaign performance. In IT, they monitored metrics related to system uptime, incident response times, and cybersecurity incidents. In manufacturing, they tracked metrics such as production efficiency, defect rates, and safety incidents.

As the dashboards took shape, Michael could sense a palpable sense of anticipation in the room. The team recognized the power of real-time tracking to drive performance improvement and were fully committed to leveraging this tool to its fullest potential.

Finally, on a bright afternoon, Michael convened a meeting to unveil the completed performance dashboards. The room buzzed with excitement as Karen presented the dynamic displays on the screen, each dashboard tailored to the specific needs of each department.

"These performance dashboards represent a significant milestone in our journey towards financial excellence," Michael declared, his voice filled with pride. "They provide us with the visibility and insight we need to make informed decisions and drive continuous improvement across the organization."

As the team absorbed the details of the performance dashboards, a sense of empowerment filled the room once again. They knew that these dashboards would enable them to track their progress in real-time, identify opportunities for improvement, and take decisive actions to achieve their strategic objectives.

With the performance dashboards in place, GlobalTech was poised to embark on the next phase of its journey towards financial excellence. As Michael looked around the room at his team, he felt a deep sense of gratitude and optimism. They had embraced real-time tracking as a strategic tool for driving performance improvement with enthusiasm and dedication, and together, they were ready to chart a course towards a brighter future.

The Positive Impact on Employee Morale and Productivity

As the performance dashboards went live at GlobalTech, Michael observed a remarkable shift in the company culture. The newfound transparency and accountability empowered employees at all levels to take ownership of their performance, leading to a tangible increase in morale and productivity.

One morning, Michael strolled through the bustling office, greeted by the sight of employees engrossed in their work, their faces alight with purpose and determination. The atmosphere was charged with energy, a stark contrast to the subdued demeanor that had prevailed before the implementation of the performance dashboards.

As he made his way to the break room, Michael overheard snippets of conversation that spoke volumes about the impact of the dashboards on employee morale.

"I love being able to see how our team's efforts contribute to the company's overall goals," one employee remarked to a colleague. "It makes me feel like what I do really matters."

"Exactly," the colleague replied, nodding enthusiastically. "And having real-time visibility into our performance keeps us all accountable and motivated to do our best."

In the break room, Michael found a group of employees gathered around one of the performance dashboards, their expressions a mix of curiosity and pride as they explored its various features.

"This dashboard is amazing," one employee exclaimed, pointing to a graph that displayed their team's progress towards a key metric. "It's so motivating to see how we're tracking against our targets in real-time."

CHAPTER 5: PERFORMANCE MEASUREMENT BREAKTHROUGHS

Another employee chimed in, "And I love that it highlights areas where we need to improve. It gives us a clear roadmap for how we can contribute to the company's success."

Michael smiled as he watched the interaction, his heart swelling with pride. The performance dashboards had not only provided valuable insights into GlobalTech's performance but had also sparked a cultural transformation, fostering a sense of ownership, accountability, and collaboration among employees.

Over the following weeks, Michael noticed a tangible increase in productivity across the organization. Teams were more focused, more engaged, and more determined to achieve their goals. Meetings were filled with lively discussions and constructive debates as employees rallied around common objectives and worked together to overcome challenges.

In the manufacturing department, productivity soared as employees leveraged the insights from the performance dashboards to streamline processes, reduce waste, and improve efficiency. In marketing, campaigns were executed with precision, driving higher conversion rates and increased customer engagement. In IT, system uptime reached record highs as teams proactively addressed issues and implemented preventive measures.

As the positive impact on employee morale and productivity became undeniable, Michael knew that the performance dashboards had become more than just a tool for tracking performance—they had become a catalyst for cultural change, driving a newfound sense of purpose and unity across the organization.

One afternoon, as he walked through the office, Michael was stopped by an employee who wanted to share their appreciation for the performance dashboards.

"I just wanted to say thank you for implementing the dashboards," the employee said, their eyes shining with sincerity. "They've made such a difference in how we work together as a team. I feel more motivated and engaged than ever before."

Michael smiled, his heart swelling with pride. "Thank you for your feedback," he replied. "I'm glad to hear that the dashboards have had a positive impact on your experience at GlobalTech. Together, we're building a culture of excellence and collaboration that will propel us towards even greater success."

As he continued on his way, Michael couldn't help but feel a sense of optimism for the future of GlobalTech. With empowered employees, a culture of accountability, and performance dashboards to guide their efforts, there was no limit to what they could achieve together.

6

Chapter 6: Strategic Management Accounting in Action

Michael's Involvement in Strategic Planning Meetings

As GlobalTech embraced strategic management accounting principles, Michael found himself at the forefront of the company's strategic planning process. His involvement in strategic planning meetings marked a pivotal moment in his career, allowing him to apply his newfound expertise to shape the company's future direction.

One crisp morning, Michael entered the boardroom, where the senior leadership team had gathered for a strategic planning session. The air hummed with anticipation as executives exchanged greetings and settled into their seats.

"Good morning, everyone," Michael greeted, his voice resonating with confidence. "I'm excited to be part of today's strategic planning meeting. Our journey towards financial excellence has given us valuable insights into our performance and opportunities for improvement. Now, it's time to translate those insights into actionable strategies that will drive our success in the years to come."

The CEO, Sandra, nodded in agreement, acknowledging Michael's contributions to the company's transformation. "Thank you, Michael," she said, her voice carrying the weight of authority. "Your expertise in strategic management accounting has been invaluable in guiding our strategic direction. Today, we'll leverage that expertise to chart a course for the future of GlobalTech."

As the meeting progressed, Michael listened intently, offering insights and recommendations based on his analysis of the company's performance and market trends. He drew upon his deep understanding of cost behavior, value creation, and performance measurement to inform the discussion and shape the strategic priorities.

"We need to focus on innovation and product development to stay ahead of the competition," Michael suggested, his tone decisive. "Investing in research and development will enable us to introduce new products and services that meet the evolving needs of our customers."

His proposal sparked a lively debate among the executives, each offering their perspectives on the best path forward. Through thoughtful discussion and analysis, they reached a consensus on the strategic priorities that would guide GlobalTech's growth and profitability in the years to come.

As the meeting concluded, Sandra turned to Michael with a grateful smile. "Thank you for your invaluable contributions today, Michael," she said. "Your insights and expertise have been instrumental in shaping our strategic direction. I look forward to seeing the impact of our decisions as we move forward."

Michael returned Sandra's smile, a sense of fulfillment swelling in his chest. His involvement in the strategic planning process had not only validated his expertise in strategic management accounting but had also cemented his role as a trusted advisor and leader within the company.

As he left the boardroom, Michael felt a renewed sense of purpose and determination. The strategic planning meeting had been a testament to the power of strategic management accounting in driving organizational success. With his guidance and expertise, GlobalTech was poised to achieve new heights of excellence and innovation in the ever-changing business landscape.

Conducting a Competitive Analysis to Identify Market Position

Following the strategic planning meeting, Michael delved into conducting a comprehensive competitive analysis to gain insights into GlobalTech's market position. Armed with strategic management accounting principles, he embarked on a journey to assess the company's strengths, weaknesses, opportunities, and threats in the competitive landscape.

With determination in his stride, Michael gathered his team in the conference room, ready to embark on the competitive analysis. The room buzzed with anticipation as they prepared to dive deep into market research and industry benchmarks.

"Good morning, everyone," Michael greeted, his voice infused with enthusiasm. "Today, we're going to conduct a competitive analysis to identify our market position and opportunities for growth. By leveraging strategic management accounting principles, we'll gain valuable insights into our competitive strengths and areas for improvement."

The team nodded in agreement, eager to get started. Michael outlined the objectives of the competitive analysis, emphasizing the importance of gathering data on key competitors, market trends, and industry benchmarks.

"We'll start by identifying our main competitors and analyzing their products, pricing strategies, and market share," Michael explained, his tone confident. "Then, we'll assess our own strengths and weaknesses relative to these competitors, identifying areas where we can differentiate ourselves and gain a competitive advantage."

As the team delved into their research, Michael led the charge, analyzing industry reports, market surveys, and financial statements to uncover insights into GlobalTech's competitive position. They assessed factors such as product quality, brand reputation, customer service, and pricing, comparing them to those of their main competitors.

In the marketing department, they analyzed competitors' marketing strategies, advertising campaigns, and customer engagement tactics to identify opportunities for improvement. In IT, they evaluated competitors' technology infrastructure, cybersecurity measures, and digital capabilities to benchmark GlobalTech's performance.

As the analysis progressed, Michael could sense a growing sense of clarity and purpose among his team. They were uncovering valuable insights into GlobalTech's market position and opportunities for growth, empowered by the strategic management accounting principles that guided their approach.

Finally, after weeks of meticulous research and analysis, Michael convened a meeting to present the findings of the competitive analysis. The room buzzed with anticipation as he displayed the key insights on the screen, highlighting GlobalTech's competitive strengths and areas for improvement.

"Our competitive analysis has provided valuable insights into our market position," Michael declared, his voice filled with pride. "We've identified opportunities for growth and areas where we can differentiate ourselves from our competitors. By leveraging these insights, we can strengthen our position in the market and drive sustainable growth."

As the team absorbed the details of the competitive analysis, a sense of determination filled the room. They knew that this strategic insight would guide their decision-making and shape their approach to capturing market opportunities.

With the competitive analysis complete, GlobalTech was poised to leverage its strengths, address its weaknesses, and capitalize on emerging opportunities in the competitive landscape. As Michael looked around the room at his team, he felt a deep sense of pride and optimism. They had embraced strategic management accounting principles with enthusiasm and dedication, and together, they were ready to chart a course towards a brighter future in the market.

Utilizing Value Chain Analysis to Enhance Operational Efficiency

With the competitive analysis providing valuable insights into GlobalTech's market position, Michael turned his focus to enhancing operational efficiency through value chain analysis. Leveraging strategic management accounting principles, he led his team in dissecting GlobalTech's value chain to identify opportunities for optimization and cost reduction.

On a bright morning, Michael gathered his team in the

conference room, the air alive with anticipation. The windows framed a picturesque view of the city skyline, a reminder of the opportunities that lay ahead.

"Good morning, everyone," Michael greeted, his voice brimming with enthusiasm. "Today, we're going to conduct a value chain analysis to enhance our operational efficiency and drive cost savings. By leveraging strategic management accounting principles, we'll identify areas where we can streamline processes and create more value for our customers."

The team nodded in agreement, eager to embark on the analysis. Michael outlined the objectives of the value chain analysis, emphasizing the importance of mapping out GlobalTech's primary and support activities to identify opportunities for improvement.

"We'll start by mapping out our value chain—from product development to customer service—and identifying the activities that create value for our customers," Michael explained, his tone confident. "Then, we'll analyze each activity to assess its cost drivers, efficiency, and contribution to our competitive advantage."

As the team delved into the analysis, Michael led the charge, guiding them through each step of the value chain. They examined processes such as product design, procurement, production, marketing, sales, and customer support, analyzing costs, timeframes, and performance metrics at each stage.

In the manufacturing department, they scrutinized production processes, supply chain management, and inventory control to identify opportunities for cost reduction and process optimization. In marketing, they evaluated advertising campaigns, brand management, and customer acquisition strategies to maximize return on investment.

CHAPTER 6: STRATEGIC MANAGEMENT ACCOUNTING IN ACTION

As the analysis progressed, Michael could sense a growing sense of clarity and purpose among his team. They were uncovering valuable insights into GlobalTech's value chain, identifying opportunities to streamline processes, eliminate waste, and enhance value for customers.

Finally, after weeks of meticulous analysis, Michael convened a meeting to present the findings of the value chain analysis. The room buzzed with anticipation as he displayed the key insights on the screen, highlighting opportunities for improvement and cost reduction.

"Our value chain analysis has provided valuable insights into our operational efficiency," Michael declared, his voice filled with pride. "We've identified opportunities to streamline processes, reduce costs, and create more value for our customers. By leveraging these insights, we can enhance our competitive advantage and drive sustainable growth."

As the team absorbed the details of the value chain analysis, a sense of determination filled the room. They knew that this strategic insight would guide their decision-making and shape their approach to operational excellence.

With the value chain analysis complete, GlobalTech was poised to optimize its operations, reduce costs, and deliver greater value to customers. As Michael looked around the room at his team, he felt a deep sense of pride and optimism. They had embraced strategic management accounting principles with enthusiasm and dedication, and together, they were ready to chart a course towards a brighter future of operational efficiency and profitability.

Applying SWOT Analysis to Business Units

With the value chain analysis shedding light on operational efficiency, Michael turned his attention to assessing the strategic position of GlobalTech's business units. Utilizing strategic management accounting principles, he led his team in conducting a SWOT analysis to identify each unit's strengths, weaknesses, opportunities, and threats, empowering them to make informed strategic decisions.

In the boardroom bathed in sunlight, Michael gathered his team once again, anticipation palpable in the air. The windows offered a sweeping view of the city below, a reminder of the vast landscape in which they operated.

"Good morning, everyone," Michael greeted, his voice filled with purpose. "Today, we're going to conduct a SWOT analysis to assess the strategic position of our business units. By leveraging strategic management accounting principles, we'll gain valuable insights into each unit's strengths, weaknesses, opportunities, and threats, enabling us to make informed decisions that drive our success."

The team nodded in agreement, ready to dive into the analysis. Michael outlined the objectives of the SWOT analysis, emphasizing the importance of evaluating internal capabilities and external factors to identify strategic priorities and mitigate risks.

"We'll start by assessing each business unit's strengths, such as market share, brand reputation, and competitive advantage," Michael explained, his tone decisive. "Then, we'll analyze their weaknesses, such as operational inefficiencies, resource constraints, and market vulnerabilities."

As the team delved into the analysis, Michael guided them

through each step of the SWOT process. They examined factors such as market trends, customer preferences, technological advancements, regulatory changes, and competitive dynamics, evaluating their impact on each business unit's strategic position.

In the marketing department, they scrutinized brand equity, customer loyalty, and product differentiation to identify opportunities for growth and market expansion. In R&D, they evaluated innovation capabilities, intellectual property, and research pipelines to capitalize on emerging trends and technologies.

As the analysis progressed, Michael could sense a growing sense of clarity and insight among his team. They were uncovering valuable insights into each business unit's strategic position, identifying opportunities to leverage strengths, address weaknesses, capitalize on opportunities, and mitigate threats.

Finally, after weeks of meticulous analysis, Michael convened a meeting to present the findings of the SWOT analysis. The room buzzed with anticipation as he displayed the key insights on the screen, highlighting each business unit's strategic priorities and areas for improvement.

"Our SWOT analysis has provided valuable insights into the strategic position of our business units," Michael declared, his voice filled with pride. "We've identified opportunities to leverage our strengths, address our weaknesses, capitalize on opportunities, and mitigate threats. By leveraging these insights, we can optimize our strategic approach and drive sustainable growth."

As the team absorbed the details of the SWOT analysis, a sense of determination filled the room. They knew that this strategic insight would guide their decision-making and shape their approach to maximizing the value of each business unit.

With the SWOT analysis complete, GlobalTech was poised to capitalize on its strengths, address its weaknesses, seize opportunities, and navigate threats in the ever-changing business landscape. As Michael looked around the room at his team, he felt a deep sense of pride and optimism. They had embraced strategic management accounting principles with enthusiasm and dedication, and together, they were ready to chart a course towards a brighter future of strategic success and sustainable growth.

Formulating Pricing Strategies Based on Cost Data

With a thorough understanding of GlobalTech's operational efficiency and strategic position, Michael set his sights on formulating pricing strategies that would maximize profitability and competitive advantage. Leveraging strategic management accounting principles, he led his team in analyzing cost data to inform pricing decisions and drive revenue growth.

In the boardroom, bathed in the warm glow of morning light, Michael gathered his team once again, their faces filled with anticipation. The windows framed a panoramic view of the city skyline, a reminder of the vast market in which they operated.

"Good morning, everyone," Michael greeted, his voice brimming with determination. "Today, we're going to formulate pricing strategies based on cost data to drive revenue growth and maximize profitability. By leveraging strategic management accounting principles, we'll gain valuable insights into our cost structure and market dynamics, enabling us to set prices that reflect the value we deliver to our customers."

The team nodded in agreement, eager to dive into the analysis. Michael outlined the objectives of the pricing strategy formulation, emphasizing the importance of aligning prices with costs, value proposition, and competitive positioning.

"We'll start by analyzing our cost data to understand the full cost of producing and delivering our products and services," Michael explained, his tone confident. "Then, we'll assess market demand, competitor pricing, and customer preferences to determine the optimal pricing strategy for each product and market segment."

As the team delved into the analysis, Michael guided them through each step of the process. They examined direct costs, such as materials, labor, and overhead, as well as indirect costs, such as marketing, distribution, and administrative expenses, to calculate the total cost of each product and service.

In the marketing department, they analyzed pricing elasticity, customer segmentation, and willingness to pay to identify pricing opportunities and challenges. In sales, they evaluated competitor pricing, market share, and customer feedback to develop pricing strategies that would capture market value and drive revenue growth.

As the analysis progressed, Michael could sense a growing sense of clarity and insight among his team. They were uncovering valuable insights into the relationship between costs, prices, and value, identifying opportunities to optimize pricing strategies and enhance profitability.

Finally, after weeks of meticulous analysis, Michael convened a meeting to present the findings of the pricing strategy formulation. The room buzzed with anticipation as he displayed the key insights on the screen, highlighting pricing recommendations for each product and market segment.

"Our pricing strategy formulation has provided valuable insights into our cost structure and market dynamics," Michael declared, his voice filled with pride. "We've identified opportunities to align prices with costs, value proposition, and competitive positioning, enabling us to drive revenue growth and maximize profitability."

As the team absorbed the details of the pricing strategy formulation, a sense of determination filled the room. They knew that this strategic insight would guide their decision-making and shape their approach to pricing in a competitive market.

With the pricing strategy formulation complete, GlobalTech was poised to set prices that reflected the value they delivered to customers, while maximizing profitability and competitive advantage. As Michael looked around the room at his team, he felt a deep sense of pride and optimism. They had embraced strategic management accounting principles with enthusiasm and dedication, and together, they were ready to chart a course towards a brighter future of strategic success and sustainable growth.

Presenting Strategic Insights to Senior Management

Armed with a wealth of strategic insights gleaned from thorough analysis and meticulous planning, Michael prepared to present his findings to the senior management team at GlobalTech. With confidence and clarity, he would articulate the path forward, leveraging strategic management accounting principles to drive the company towards its goals of growth and profitability.

CHAPTER 6: STRATEGIC MANAGEMENT ACCOUNTING IN ACTION

In the boardroom, bathed in the soft glow of morning light, Michael stood at the head of the table, his team gathered around him, their faces reflecting a mix of anticipation and determination. The windows framed a sweeping view of the city skyline, a reminder of the vast opportunities that lay ahead.

"Good morning, everyone," Michael began, his voice steady and commanding. "Today, I'm excited to present our strategic insights, informed by rigorous analysis and strategic management accounting principles. These insights will guide our decisions and actions as we chart a course towards sustainable growth and profitability."

He proceeded to outline the key findings of their analysis, starting with an overview of GlobalTech's operational efficiency, strategic position, and market dynamics. With clarity and precision, he articulated the opportunities for growth and the challenges that lay ahead, painting a vivid picture of the company's strategic landscape.

"As we look to the future, it's clear that we have significant opportunities to leverage our strengths, address our weaknesses, and capitalize on emerging trends," Michael explained, his tone confident. "By aligning our strategies with market dynamics and customer needs, we can position GlobalTech for long-term success."

He then delved into the specific recommendations arising from their analysis, ranging from operational improvements to pricing strategies to market expansion initiatives. Each recommendation was grounded in data and supported by strategic rationale, designed to drive value creation and competitive advantage.

"As we move forward, it's essential that we remain agile and adaptable in the face of change," Michael emphasized, his gaze sweeping across the room. "By leveraging strategic management accounting principles, we can make informed decisions that drive our success and ensure a prosperous future for GlobalTech."

As Michael concluded his presentation, the room fell silent, the weight of his words hanging in the air. The senior management team absorbed the insights he had shared, recognizing the depth of analysis and strategic vision that had gone into their development.

Finally, Sandra, the CEO, broke the silence, her voice filled with admiration and gratitude. "Thank you, Michael, for your outstanding presentation," she said, her tone warm and appreciative. "Your strategic insights are invaluable in guiding our decisions and shaping our future direction. I have no doubt that with your leadership, GlobalTech will achieve great things."

As the meeting adjourned, Michael felt a sense of satisfaction wash over him. His presentation had resonated with the senior management team, laying the foundation for future success. With strategic management accounting principles as their guide, GlobalTech was poised to navigate the complexities of the business landscape and emerge stronger and more resilient than ever before.

7

Chapter 7: Navigating Capital Budgeting Decisions

Introduction to Capital Budgeting Techniques

As GlobalTech continued its journey towards financial excellence, Michael embarked on navigating capital budgeting decisions, a critical aspect of strategic financial management. With the goal of maximizing long-term value creation, he led his team in exploring various capital budgeting techniques to guide investment decisions and allocate resources effectively.

In the conference room, bathed in the soft glow of morning light, Michael stood before his team, their faces reflecting a mix of curiosity and determination. The windows offered a panoramic view of the city skyline, a reminder of the vast opportunities that awaited them.

"Good morning, everyone," Michael began, his voice projecting confidence and authority. "Today, we're going to explore the world of capital budgeting, a fundamental aspect of strategic financial management. By leveraging capital budgeting techniques, we can evaluate investment opportunities, allocate resources efficiently, and maximize long-term value creation for GlobalTech."

He proceeded to outline the objectives of the session, starting with an overview of capital budgeting and its importance in strategic decision-making. With clarity and precision, he explained the role of capital budgeting techniques in evaluating potential investments and assessing their impact on the company's financial performance.

"As we consider investment opportunities, it's essential that we use capital budgeting techniques to make informed decisions that align with our strategic objectives," Michael explained, his tone authoritative. "These techniques provide us with the tools and frameworks we need to evaluate the costs, benefits, and risks associated with each investment opportunity."

He then delved into the various capital budgeting techniques, including:

1. **Net Present Value (NPV)**: Evaluating the present value of future cash flows associated with an investment, taking into account the time value of money and the cost of capital.
2. **Internal Rate of Return (IRR)**: Determining the discount rate at which the net present value of an investment is zero, providing insights into the project's potential return on investment.
3. **Payback Period**: Calculating the time it takes for an investment to recoup its initial cost through the net cash flows it generates.

4. **Profitability Index (PI)**: Assessing the ratio of the present value of future cash flows to the initial investment, helping to prioritize investment opportunities based on their potential return relative to their cost.

"As we navigate capital budgeting decisions, it's important to consider the unique characteristics of each investment opportunity and select the most appropriate technique for evaluation," Michael emphasized, his gaze sweeping across the room. "By leveraging these techniques effectively, we can make sound investment decisions that drive long-term value creation for GlobalTech."

As the team absorbed the details of the introduction to capital budgeting techniques, a sense of determination filled the room. They knew that mastering these techniques would enable them to evaluate investment opportunities with rigor and precision, guiding GlobalTech towards sustainable growth and financial success.

Assessing Potential Investment Projects using NPV and IRR

With the foundation of capital budgeting techniques laid out, Michael led his team in a deep dive into assessing potential investment projects using two key methods: Net Present Value (NPV) and Internal Rate of Return (IRR). Armed with these tools, they would evaluate investment opportunities with precision and confidence, ensuring that GlobalTech allocated its resources effectively for maximum long-term value creation.

In the conference room, the atmosphere crackled with

anticipation as Michael stood before his team once again. The windows framed a vibrant cityscape, a backdrop to the strategic decisions that would shape GlobalTech's future.

"Good morning, everyone," Michael greeted, his voice filled with energy. "Today, we're going to put our knowledge of capital budgeting techniques into action by assessing potential investment projects using NPV and IRR. These methods will allow us to evaluate the financial viability of each project and determine their impact on GlobalTech's long-term profitability."

He began by presenting the team with a series of investment opportunities, ranging from research and development initiatives to new product launches to infrastructure upgrades. Each opportunity was accompanied by a detailed financial analysis, including projected cash flows, initial investment costs, and discount rates.

"As we assess these investment opportunities, our goal is to determine whether they generate positive NPV and meet our internal rate of return hurdle rate," Michael explained, his tone focused. "A positive NPV indicates that the project is expected to increase the value of the company, while meeting our IRR hurdle rate ensures that the project generates a return on investment that exceeds our cost of capital."

The team immersed themselves in the analysis, crunching numbers and scrutinizing assumptions with meticulous attention to detail. They inputted cash flow projections into spreadsheets, calculated NPV and IRR for each investment opportunity, and compared the results against predetermined thresholds to determine their financial feasibility.

As the analysis unfolded, Michael guided his team through the intricacies of NPV and IRR, illustrating their importance in evaluating investment decisions with real-world examples and case studies. He emphasized the need to consider factors such as risk, timing, and opportunity costs when interpreting the results and making recommendations.

"As we review the results of our analysis, it's important to remember that NPV and IRR are powerful tools, but they are not the only factors to consider," Michael reminded them, his voice measured. "We must also assess qualitative factors such as strategic alignment, market demand, and competitive dynamics to ensure that our investment decisions are sound and aligned with our long-term objectives."

After hours of intense analysis and discussion, the team emerged with a clear understanding of the potential investment projects' financial implications. Armed with the insights gleaned from NPV and IRR analysis, they were ready to make informed recommendations that would drive GlobalTech's growth and profitability in the years to come.

As the meeting concluded, Michael felt a sense of pride in his team's accomplishments. By mastering NPV and IRR, they had unlocked the power to evaluate investment opportunities with rigor and precision, ensuring that GlobalTech allocated its resources effectively to maximize long-term value creation.

Collaborating with the Finance Team for Accurate Projections

Recognizing the critical importance of accurate financial projections in capital budgeting decisions, Michael knew that collaboration with the finance team was essential. Together, they would ensure that the projected cash flows and investment costs were meticulously calculated, providing a solid foundation for evaluating potential investment projects and guiding GlobalTech towards financial success.

In the bustling finance department, Michael convened a meeting with the finance team, their expertise in financial analysis and modeling invaluable for the task at hand. The room buzzed with focused energy as they prepared to delve into the intricacies of forecasting and budgeting.

"Good morning, everyone," Michael greeted, his tone conveying both warmth and determination. "Today, we're going to collaborate on refining the financial projections for our potential investment projects. By leveraging your expertise in financial analysis and modeling, we can ensure that our projections are accurate and reliable, providing us with a solid foundation for our capital budgeting decisions."

The finance team nodded in agreement, eager to contribute their skills to the process. Michael outlined the objectives of the collaboration, emphasizing the importance of aligning the projections with industry benchmarks, historical data, and macroeconomic trends to ensure their accuracy and relevance.

"We'll start by reviewing the assumptions and inputs used in our financial models," Michael explained, his voice clear and concise. "We'll then work together to refine these assumptions based on the latest market data and insights, ensuring that our projections are as accurate and realistic as possible."

As they delved into the financial projections, the team's expertise shone through, each member contributing their unique insights and perspectives to the process. They analyzed factors such as revenue growth rates, cost structures, pricing dynamics, and capital expenditure requirements, meticulously calibrating their models to reflect the nuances of each investment opportunity.

"Accuracy and attention to detail are paramount in our projections," Michael reminded the team, his gaze sweeping across the room. "We need to ensure that our assumptions are grounded in reality and that our models are robust enough to withstand scrutiny and uncertainty."

With hours of intense collaboration behind them, the finance team emerged with refined financial projections that served as the bedrock for GlobalTech's capital budgeting decisions. Each projection was meticulously crafted, incorporating the latest market data and insights to provide a comprehensive view of the potential investment projects' financial implications.

As the meeting concluded, Michael expressed his gratitude to the finance team for their dedication and expertise. Together, they had laid the groundwork for informed capital budgeting decisions, ensuring that GlobalTech allocated its resources effectively and responsibly to drive long-term value creation and financial success.

With accurate projections in hand, GlobalTech was poised to evaluate potential investment projects with confidence and precision, leveraging the insights gleaned from collaboration with the finance team to guide its strategic decision-making and secure its position as a leader in the industry.

Presenting Investment Proposals to the Board

With accurate financial projections and thorough analysis in hand, Michael prepared to present the investment proposals to the board of directors. This pivotal moment would determine the allocation of resources and shape the future direction of GlobalTech. With poise and confidence, Michael stood ready to articulate the strategic rationale behind each proposal, guiding the board towards decisions that would drive the company's growth and prosperity.

In the grand boardroom, bathed in the soft glow of morning light, Michael stood at the head of the table, the board of directors assembled before him. The air hummed with anticipation as he prepared to unveil the investment proposals that would shape GlobalTech's future.

"Good morning, esteemed board members," Michael began, his voice projecting confidence and authority. "Today, I am excited to present our investment proposals, informed by rigorous analysis and strategic vision. These proposals represent strategic opportunities for GlobalTech to enhance its competitive position, drive growth, and create long-term value for our shareholders."

He proceeded to outline the objectives of the presentation, starting with an overview of the investment opportunities and their alignment with GlobalTech's strategic priorities. With clarity and precision, he articulated the strategic rationale behind each proposal, highlighting the anticipated benefits and potential risks.

"As we evaluate these investment opportunities, it's important to consider their potential impact on GlobalTech's financial performance and long-term value creation," Michael explained, his tone focused. "Each proposal has undergone thorough analysis, including detailed financial projections, sensitivity analysis, and risk assessment, to ensure that it aligns with our strategic objectives and generates a positive return on investment."

He then delved into the specifics of each proposal, presenting the projected cash flows, investment costs, and expected returns for the board's consideration. With each slide, he painted a vivid picture of the opportunities that lay ahead, backed by robust financial analysis and strategic rationale.

"As stewards of GlobalTech's resources, it is our responsibility to make informed decisions that maximize shareholder value and ensure the company's long-term success," Michael emphasized, his gaze sweeping across the room. "These investment proposals have been carefully crafted to position GlobalTech for growth and profitability in the years to come."

As the presentation concluded, the board members exchanged thoughtful glances, their minds buzzing with possibilities. Michael's strategic insights had resonated with them, laying the groundwork for thoughtful deliberation and decisive action.

After a brief moment of reflection, the chairman of the board rose to speak, his voice filled with conviction. "Thank you, Michael, for your insightful presentation," he said, addressing the room. "These investment proposals represent exciting opportunities for GlobalTech to drive growth and create value. Let us now deliberate carefully and make decisions that will propel our company towards a bright and prosperous future."

As the board adjourned to deliberate, Michael felt a sense of satisfaction wash over him. His presentation had set the stage for strategic decisions that would shape GlobalTech's trajectory in the years to come. With sound investment proposals and a clear vision for the future, GlobalTech was poised to seize opportunities, navigate challenges, and emerge stronger and more resilient than ever before.

Case Study: A Successful Investment and Its Impact on the Company

As GlobalTech's investment proposals awaited the board's deliberation, Michael took the opportunity to showcase a case study of a previous successful investment. This real-life example would illustrate the tangible benefits of strategic capital allocation and provide the board with confidence in their decision-making process.

In the intimate setting of the executive conference room, Michael began his presentation, the board members leaning in with interest. The atmosphere was charged with anticipation as he prepared to unveil the success story that awaited them.

"Good morning, esteemed board members," Michael greeted, his voice filled with enthusiasm. "Today, I am excited to share with you a case study of a successful investment that has had a transformative impact on GlobalTech's performance and profitability."

He proceeded to outline the details of the investment, a strategic acquisition that had expanded GlobalTech's product portfolio and enhanced its competitive position in the market. With clarity and precision, he described the rationale behind the investment, highlighting the synergies, opportunities, and strategic value it had brought to the company.

"As we reflect on this case study, it's clear that strategic capital allocation is crucial for driving long-term value creation,"

Michael explained, his tone confident. "By investing in opportunities that align with our strategic objectives and create synergies with our existing business lines, we can unlock new growth avenues and solidify our position as a leader in the industry."

He then delved into the impact of the investment on GlobalTech's financial performance, presenting key metrics such as revenue growth, profit margins, and market share. With each slide, he painted a compelling picture of the investment's success, backed by tangible results and measurable outcomes.

"Since the acquisition, GlobalTech has experienced significant growth and expansion, with revenues increasing by X% and profit margins expanding by Y%," Michael revealed, his voice resonating with pride. "This success story is a testament to the power of strategic capital allocation and the value it can create for our shareholders."

As the presentation concluded, the board members exchanged impressed glances, their confidence in GlobalTech's strategic direction bolstered by the success of the case study. Michael's insights had illuminated the path forward, demonstrating the potential for strategic investments to drive growth, profitability, and shareholder value.

After a moment of reflection, the chairman of the board rose to speak, his voice filled with admiration. "Thank you, Michael, for sharing this inspiring case study with us," he said, addressing the room. "It is clear that strategic capital allocation is a cornerstone of our success, and I have no doubt that the investment proposals before us will follow in the footsteps of this successful endeavor."

As the board members nodded in agreement, Michael felt a sense of satisfaction wash over him. His case study had resonated with them, providing tangible evidence of the transformative impact that strategic investments could have on GlobalTech's performance and profitability. With confidence in their decision-making process, the board was ready to chart a course towards a future filled with growth, prosperity, and success.

Michael's Personal Growth from Managing High-Stakes Decisions

As Michael reflected on the journey of navigating capital budgeting decisions and presenting investment proposals to the board, he couldn't help but recognize the profound personal growth he had experienced throughout the process. Managing high-stakes decisions had challenged him to push past his comfort zone, embrace uncertainty, and lead with confidence and conviction.

Alone in his office, Michael took a moment to pause and reflect on the lessons he had learned along the way. The room was bathed in the soft glow of lamplight, casting a sense of tranquility over the space as he allowed his thoughts to wander.

"Managing high-stakes decisions has been a journey of growth and discovery," Michael mused, his voice filled with introspection. "It has challenged me to step outside of my comfort zone, confront uncertainty, and trust in my abilities as a leader."

He recalled the moments of doubt and hesitation that had punctuated his journey, the weight of responsibility bearing down on his shoulders as he navigated complex financial decisions and presented investment proposals to the board. Each decision had been fraught with risk, yet filled with the potential for growth and opportunity.

"As I reflect on the challenges we've faced and the decisions we've made, I'm reminded of the importance of resilience and perseverance," Michael continued, his tone contemplative. "Managing high-stakes decisions requires courage, determination, and a willingness to embrace failure as a stepping stone to success."

He thought back to the times when he had been pushed to the brink, grappling with uncertainty and adversity as he sought to navigate the complexities of capital budgeting and strategic decision-making. Each obstacle had tested his resolve, yet ultimately strengthened his resolve and fortified his character.

"As I stand here today, I am grateful for the opportunities I've had to grow and evolve as a leader," Michael reflected, a sense of gratitude washing over him. "Managing high-stakes decisions has been a transformative experience, shaping me into a more confident, resilient, and visionary leader."

With a renewed sense of purpose and determination, Michael turned his gaze towards the future, ready to embrace the challenges and opportunities that lay ahead. Armed with the lessons learned from managing high-stakes decisions, he was poised to lead GlobalTech towards a future filled with growth, prosperity, and success.

8

Chapter 8: Optimizing Working Capital

Analyzing the Company's Current Working Capital Management

As GlobalTech continued its journey towards financial excellence, Michael turned his attention to optimizing working capital, a critical aspect of financial management that could unlock liquidity, improve cash flow, and enhance operational efficiency. With a keen eye for detail and a commitment to continuous improvement, he led his team in analyzing the company's current working capital management practices to identify opportunities for optimization and efficiency gains.

In the bustling conference room, Michael gathered his team, their faces reflecting a mix of anticipation and determination. The air was charged with energy as they prepared to delve into the intricacies of working capital management.

"Good morning, everyone," Michael greeted, his voice brimming with enthusiasm. "Today, we're going to analyze the company's current working capital management practices to identify opportunities for optimization and efficiency gains. By streamlining our processes and enhancing our controls, we can unlock liquidity, improve cash flow, and drive operational efficiency for GlobalTech."

He began by outlining the objectives of the analysis, emphasizing the importance of understanding the components of working capital and their impact on the company's financial health. With clarity and precision, he explained the role of working capital in financing day-to-day operations, managing liquidity, and supporting growth initiatives.

"As we analyze the company's current working capital management practices, it's important to consider each component of working capital, including accounts receivable, accounts payable, and inventory," Michael explained, his tone focused. "By identifying areas of inefficiency and implementing targeted strategies for improvement, we can optimize our working capital position and strengthen our financial resilience."

He then delved into the specifics of the analysis, examining key metrics such as the cash conversion cycle, days sales outstanding (DSO), days payable outstanding (DPO), and inventory turnover ratio. With each metric, he provided insights into the company's performance relative to industry benchmarks and best practices, identifying areas of strength and opportunities for improvement.

"As we review the data, it's clear that there are opportunities for optimization across the board," Michael observed, his gaze sweeping across the room. "From streamlining our accounts receivable processes to optimizing our inventory management practices, there are numerous ways we can enhance our working capital management and drive value for GlobalTech."

As the team immersed themselves in the analysis, a sense of purpose filled the room. They knew that by optimizing working capital, they could unlock liquidity, improve cash flow, and enhance operational efficiency, positioning GlobalTech for sustainable growth and financial success.

With the analysis underway, Michael and his team embarked on a journey of discovery and optimization, determined to unlock the full potential of working capital and drive value creation for GlobalTech in the years to come.

Implementing Cash Management Strategies

With a thorough analysis of the company's current working capital management practices complete, Michael shifted his focus to implementing cash management strategies aimed at optimizing liquidity and improving cash flow. Recognizing the importance of effective cash management in driving financial stability and resilience, he led his team in developing and implementing targeted strategies to enhance GlobalTech's cash position.

In the strategic planning room, Michael gathered his team once again, the atmosphere charged with anticipation as they prepared to delve into the intricacies of cash management.

"Good morning, everyone," Michael greeted, his voice filled with determination. "Today, we're going to implement cash management strategies aimed at optimizing liquidity and improving cash flow for GlobalTech. By maximizing our cash resources and minimizing idle balances, we can strengthen our financial resilience and support our growth initiatives."

He began by outlining the objectives of the cash management

strategies, emphasizing the importance of balancing liquidity needs with investment opportunities and debt obligations. With clarity and precision, he explained the role of cash management in maintaining operational stability, meeting financial commitments, and seizing strategic opportunities.

"As we implement these strategies, it's important to strike the right balance between liquidity and profitability," Michael explained, his tone focused. "By optimizing our cash resources and minimizing financing costs, we can improve our financial flexibility and position GlobalTech for long-term success."

He then delved into the specifics of the strategies, including:

1. **Cash Forecasting**: Developing accurate cash forecasts to anticipate cash inflows and outflows, allowing for proactive cash management and effective liquidity planning.
2. **Working Capital Optimization**: Streamlining accounts receivable, accounts payable, and inventory management processes to reduce working capital requirements and free up cash for strategic initiatives.
3. **Short-Term Investments**: Identifying opportunities for short-term investments to optimize cash balances and maximize returns on excess cash reserves.

"As we implement these strategies, it's essential that we maintain strong internal controls and adhere to best practices in cash management," Michael emphasized, his gaze sweeping across the room. "By fostering a culture of accountability and transparency, we can ensure the integrity of our cash management processes and safeguard GlobalTech's financial assets."

As the team absorbed the details of the cash management

strategies, a sense of determination filled the room. They knew that by implementing these strategies effectively, they could optimize GlobalTech's cash position, improve cash flow, and enhance the company's financial resilience in an ever-changing business environment.

With the strategies in motion, Michael and his team embarked on a journey of proactive cash management, confident in their ability to optimize liquidity, improve cash flow, and position GlobalTech for sustainable growth and success in the years to come.

Improving Inventory Management Systems

As Michael and his team continued their quest to optimize working capital, they turned their attention to improving inventory management systems. Recognizing that efficient inventory management was crucial for controlling costs, minimizing excess inventory, and maximizing cash flow, they embarked on a journey to streamline processes and enhance efficiency.

In the innovation hub of GlobalTech, Michael gathered his team once more, the air filled with anticipation as they prepared to tackle the complexities of inventory management.

"Good morning, everyone," Michael greeted, his voice resonating with determination. "Today, we're going to improve our inventory management systems to control costs, minimize excess inventory, and optimize cash flow for GlobalTech. By implementing best practices and leveraging technology, we can enhance efficiency and drive value for our company."

He began by outlining the objectives of the inventory management improvement initiative, emphasizing the importance of balancing inventory levels with customer demand and production capabilities. With clarity and precision, he explained the role of inventory management in supporting operational efficiency, reducing carrying costs, and improving customer satisfaction.

"As we improve our inventory management systems, it's crucial that we strike the right balance between inventory levels and service levels," Michael explained, his tone focused. "By optimizing our inventory turnover ratio and reducing stockouts and excess inventory, we can improve cash flow and profitability for GlobalTech."

He then delved into the specifics of the improvement initiative, including:

1. **Demand Forecasting**: Utilizing advanced forecasting techniques and data analytics to predict customer demand more accurately, allowing for better inventory planning and replenishment.
2. **Just-in-Time (JIT) Inventory**: Implementing JIT inventory practices to minimize excess inventory and reduce carrying costs, while ensuring timely delivery of products to customers.
3. **Inventory Optimization Software**: Investing in inventory optimization software to automate replenishment processes, optimize stock levels, and reduce the risk of stockouts and overstock situations.

"As we implement these improvements, it's important to foster collaboration between our procurement, production, and sales teams," Michael emphasized, his gaze sweeping across the room. "By aligning our inventory management practices with customer demand and production schedules, we can improve efficiency and responsiveness throughout the supply chain."

As the team absorbed the details of the inventory management improvement initiative, a sense of purpose filled the room. They knew that by implementing these changes effectively, they could optimize inventory levels, reduce costs, and improve cash flow for GlobalTech, positioning the company for long-term success in a competitive market.

With the improvement initiative underway, Michael and his team embarked on a journey of continuous improvement, confident in their ability to enhance efficiency and drive value through streamlined inventory management systems.

Streamlining Receivables and Payables Processes

With the quest to optimize working capital in full swing, Michael turned his attention to streamlining receivables and payables processes. Recognizing the critical importance of efficient cash conversion cycles in maintaining liquidity and maximizing cash flow, he led his team in implementing strategies to accelerate collections, optimize payment terms, and improve overall cash management efficiency.

In the collaborative space of GlobalTech's finance department, Michael convened his team once again, the air buzzing with anticipation as they prepared to tackle the complexities of receivables and payables management.

"Good morning, everyone," Michael greeted, his voice imbued with determination. "Today, we're going to streamline our receivables and payables processes to accelerate collections, optimize payment terms, and improve cash flow for GlobalTech. By enhancing efficiency and reducing payment delays, we can unlock liquidity and drive value for our company."

He began by outlining the objectives of the initiative, emphasizing the importance of minimizing the cash conversion cycle and maximizing working capital efficiency. With clarity and precision, he explained the role of receivables and payables management in supporting cash flow, managing liquidity, and strengthening financial resilience.

"As we streamline our receivables and payables processes, it's crucial that we focus on improving efficiency without compromising relationships with customers and suppliers," Michael explained, his tone focused. "By optimizing payment terms and collections processes, we can improve cash flow and operational efficiency while maintaining strong partnerships throughout the supply chain."

He then delved into the specifics of the initiative, including:

1. **Customer Credit Policies**: Reviewing and refining customer credit policies to minimize credit risk and reduce the incidence of late payments, while ensuring that sales opportunities are not lost.
2. **Accounts Receivable Automation**: Implementing automated receivables management systems to streamline invoicing, collections, and reconciliation processes, reducing administrative overhead and accelerating cash inflows.
3. **Vendor Negotiations**: Engaging in proactive negotiations with vendors to optimize payment terms, extend payment cycles, and improve cash flow management, while maintaining positive supplier relationships.

"As we implement these strategies, it's important to foster collaboration between our sales, finance, and procurement teams," Michael emphasized, his gaze sweeping across the room. "By aligning our receivables and payables processes with business objectives and market dynamics, we can enhance efficiency and drive value throughout the organization."

As the team absorbed the details of the initiative, a sense of purpose filled the room. They knew that by implementing these changes effectively, they could optimize cash flow, improve liquidity, and strengthen financial resilience for GlobalTech, positioning the company for sustainable growth and success in a dynamic business environment.

With the initiative underway, Michael and his team embarked on a journey of continuous improvement, confident in their ability to drive value through streamlined receivables and payables processes, and to further optimize working capital to support GlobalTech's strategic objectives.

The Introduction of Working Capital Financing Options

As GlobalTech pursued its mission to optimize working capital, Michael recognized the importance of exploring financing options to support the company's liquidity needs and capital requirements. With a strategic focus on balancing internal cash generation with external financing sources, he led his team in exploring and introducing working capital financing options tailored to GlobalTech's unique needs and circumstances.

In the boardroom, Michael gathered his team once again, the atmosphere filled with anticipation as they prepared to delve into the intricacies of working capital financing.

"Good morning, everyone," Michael greeted, his voice filled

with determination. "Today, we're going to explore working capital financing options to support GlobalTech's liquidity needs and capital requirements. By leveraging a mix of internal cash generation and external financing sources, we can optimize our working capital position and drive value for our company."

He began by outlining the objectives of the initiative, emphasizing the importance of aligning financing options with GlobalTech's strategic objectives and financial priorities. With clarity and precision, he explained the role of working capital financing in supporting growth initiatives, managing liquidity, and optimizing capital structure.

"As we explore working capital financing options, it's crucial that we assess each option's costs, risks, and benefits," Michael explained, his tone focused. "By selecting the right mix of financing sources, we can optimize our capital structure and ensure that we have the necessary resources to support our strategic objectives."

He then delved into the specifics of the financing options, including:

1. **Revolving Lines of Credit**: Exploring the use of revolving lines of credit to provide short-term financing for working capital needs, allowing for flexibility and responsiveness to changing business conditions.
2. **Invoice Financing**: Considering invoice financing options to monetize accounts receivable and unlock liquidity, providing immediate cash flow relief without adding additional debt to the balance sheet.
3. **Supply Chain Finance**: Evaluating supply chain finance programs to optimize payment terms with suppliers and

improve working capital efficiency, while strengthening relationships throughout the supply chain.

"As we introduce these financing options, it's important to maintain a disciplined approach to capital management," Michael emphasized, his gaze sweeping across the room. "By carefully managing our cash flow and debt obligations, we can ensure that we maintain financial stability and flexibility while pursuing growth opportunities."

As the team absorbed the details of the financing options, a sense of anticipation filled the room. They knew that by introducing these options effectively, they could optimize working capital, improve liquidity, and support GlobalTech's strategic objectives, positioning the company for sustainable growth and success in a dynamic business environment.

With the financing options on the table, Michael and his team embarked on a journey of strategic capital management, confident in their ability to optimize working capital and drive value for GlobalTech in the years to come.

Tangible Benefits Seen in the Company's Liquidity and Efficiency

After implementing a comprehensive suite of strategies to optimize working capital, Michael and his team began to see tangible benefits manifest in the company's liquidity and efficiency. The concerted efforts to streamline processes, improve cash flow, and explore financing options had yielded positive results, strengthening GlobalTech's financial position and positioning the company for continued success.

In the executive boardroom, Michael stood before the senior

leadership team, a sense of satisfaction evident in his demeanor as he prepared to share the news of the company's progress.

"Good morning, everyone," Michael greeted, his voice filled with enthusiasm. "Today, I'm pleased to share with you the tangible benefits we've seen in the company's liquidity and efficiency as a result of our efforts to optimize working capital."

He began by highlighting the improvements in liquidity, emphasizing the increase in cash reserves and the reduction in reliance on short-term borrowing. With clarity and precision, he explained how the implementation of cash management strategies, improvements in inventory and receivables management, and the introduction of financing options had contributed to the strengthening of GlobalTech's liquidity position.

"As a result of these initiatives, we've seen a significant improvement in our cash flow and liquidity metrics," Michael explained, his tone confident. "Our cash reserves have increased by X%, and our reliance on short-term borrowing has decreased by Y%, providing us with greater financial flexibility and stability."

He then shifted his focus to the improvements in efficiency, highlighting the reduction in the cash conversion cycle and the increase in working capital turnover. With each metric, he provided insights into how the streamlining of processes, automation of workflows, and optimization of payment terms had contributed to the enhancement of GlobalTech's operational efficiency.

"As a result of our efforts to optimize working capital, we've seen a measurable improvement in our efficiency metrics," Michael continued, his gaze sweeping across the room. "Our cash conversion cycle has decreased by X days, and our working capital turnover has increased by Y%, indicating that we are utilizing our resources more effectively and generating value for the company."

As the senior leadership team absorbed the news, a sense of satisfaction filled the room. They knew that the tangible benefits seen in the company's liquidity and efficiency were a testament to the hard work and dedication of Michael and his team, and a reflection of GlobalTech's commitment to excellence in financial management.

With the company's financial position strengthened and its operational efficiency optimized, GlobalTech was well-positioned to capitalize on growth opportunities, navigate challenges, and continue its journey towards sustainable success in a dynamic and competitive market.

9

Chapter 9: Strengthening Internal Controls

Identifying Weaknesses in Current Internal Controls

As GlobalTech aimed to ensure robust financial management practices, Michael turned his attention to strengthening internal controls. Recognizing the critical importance of effective controls in safeguarding assets, mitigating risks, and ensuring compliance, he led his team in identifying weaknesses in the company's current internal control framework.

In the secure confines of GlobalTech's internal audit department, Michael convened his team, the atmosphere tinged with a sense of urgency as they prepared to address the complexities of internal controls.

"Good morning, everyone," Michael greeted, his voice filled with determination. "Today, we're going to identify weaknesses in our current internal control framework to strengthen our financial management practices and mitigate risks for

GlobalTech. By enhancing our controls, we can safeguard our assets and ensure the integrity of our financial reporting."

He began by outlining the objectives of the assessment, emphasizing the importance of identifying gaps and vulnerabilities in the company's internal control environment. With clarity and precision, he explained the role of internal controls in preventing fraud, detecting errors, and promoting operational efficiency.

"As we assess our internal control framework, it's crucial that we conduct a thorough review of key processes and control activities," Michael explained, his tone focused. "By identifying weaknesses and areas for improvement, we can implement targeted strategies to strengthen our controls and mitigate risks effectively."

He then delved into the specifics of the assessment, including:

1. **Risk Assessment**: Conducting a comprehensive risk assessment to identify potential threats and vulnerabilities across key business processes, including financial reporting, procurement, and inventory management.
2. **Control Testing**: Performing detailed testing of existing controls to evaluate their effectiveness in mitigating risks and ensuring compliance with regulatory requirements, industry standards, and company policies.
3. **Gap Analysis**: Identifying gaps and deficiencies in the current control environment, including weaknesses in segregation of duties, inadequate documentation, and insufficient monitoring and oversight.

"As we uncover weaknesses in our internal control framework, it's important to prioritize remediation efforts based on risk severity and potential impact," Michael emphasized, his gaze sweeping across the room. "By addressing these weaknesses proactively, we can enhance our controls, mitigate risks, and strengthen GlobalTech's overall governance and compliance posture."

As the team absorbed the details of the assessment, a sense of purpose filled the room. They knew that by identifying and addressing weaknesses in the company's internal control framework, they could enhance transparency, accountability, and trust in GlobalTech's financial management practices, positioning the company for long-term success in a dynamic business environment.

With the assessment underway, Michael and his team embarked on a journey of strengthening internal controls, confident in their ability to mitigate risks effectively and safeguard GlobalTech's assets and reputation in an ever-evolving landscape of regulatory requirements and business challenges.

Developing a Comprehensive Risk Assessment Framework

With weaknesses in the current internal control framework identified, Michael and his team turned their focus to developing a comprehensive risk assessment framework. Recognizing the importance of systematically identifying and prioritizing risks across key business processes, they embarked on a journey to enhance GlobalTech's risk management capabilities and ensure proactive mitigation of potential threats.

In the strategic planning room, Michael gathered his team once more, the air buzzing with anticipation as they prepared to tackle the complexities of risk assessment.

"Good morning, everyone," Michael greeted, his voice filled with determination. "Today, we're going to develop a comprehensive risk assessment framework to systematically identify and prioritize risks across key business processes for Global-Tech. By enhancing our risk management capabilities, we can strengthen our internal controls and safeguard our company's assets and reputation."

He began by outlining the objectives of the framework, emphasizing the importance of a structured approach to risk assessment in identifying potential threats and vulnerabilities. With clarity and precision, he explained the role of risk assessment in informing decision-making, resource allocation, and control design.

"As we develop this framework, it's crucial that we engage stakeholders from across the organization and leverage their expertise and insights," Michael explained, his tone focused. "By fostering collaboration and knowledge-sharing, we can ensure that our risk assessment process is comprehensive, relevant, and actionable."

He then delved into the specifics of the framework, including:

1. **Risk Identification**: Engaging stakeholders in identifying and documenting risks across key business processes, including financial reporting, operations, compliance, and information technology.
2. **Risk Evaluation**: Assessing the likelihood and potential impact of identified risks using qualitative and quantitative techniques, such as risk matrices, scenario analysis, and historical data analysis.

3. **Risk Prioritization**: Prioritizing risks based on their significance to the achievement of organizational objectives, regulatory requirements, and potential impact on the company's financial performance and reputation.

"As we develop this framework, it's important to ensure that it is flexible and adaptable to changing business conditions and emerging risks," Michael emphasized, his gaze sweeping across the room. "By continuously monitoring and updating our risk assessment process, we can stay ahead of evolving threats and proactively mitigate risks to GlobalTech's success."

As the team absorbed the details of the framework, a sense of purpose filled the room. They knew that by developing a comprehensive risk assessment framework, they could enhance GlobalTech's risk management capabilities and ensure proactive mitigation of potential threats, positioning the company for long-term success in a dynamic and uncertain business environment.

With the framework underway, Michael and his team embarked on a journey of strengthening internal controls and enhancing risk management practices, confident in their ability to safeguard GlobalTech's assets and reputation and drive value for the company in the years to come.

Implementing New Internal Control Systems

With a comprehensive risk assessment framework in place, Michael and his team shifted their focus to implementing new internal control systems. Recognizing the importance of robust controls in mitigating risks and ensuring compliance, they embarked on a journey to design and implement tailored control measures to address identified weaknesses and vulnerabilities.

In the command center of GlobalTech's internal audit department, Michael gathered his team once again, the atmosphere charged with anticipation as they prepared to roll out the new control systems.

"Good morning, everyone," Michael greeted, his voice resonating with determination. "Today, we're going to implement new internal control systems to address identified weaknesses and vulnerabilities and strengthen GlobalTech's risk management capabilities. By enhancing our controls, we can safeguard our assets and ensure the integrity of our financial reporting and operations."

He began by outlining the objectives of the implementation, emphasizing the importance of aligning control measures with the company's risk profile and strategic objectives. With clarity and precision, he explained the role of internal controls in preventing fraud, detecting errors, and promoting operational efficiency.

"As we implement these new control systems, it's crucial that we prioritize effectiveness, efficiency, and scalability," Michael explained, his tone focused. "By designing controls that are tailored to our business processes and supported by technology, we can improve compliance, enhance transparency, and mitigate risks effectively."

He then delved into the specifics of the implementation, including:

1. **Control Design**: Designing control measures to address identified risks and vulnerabilities, including segregation of duties, authorization procedures, and transaction

monitoring.
2. **Automation**: Leveraging technology to automate control activities and streamline compliance processes, reducing manual effort and improving accuracy and timeliness.
3. **Monitoring and Oversight**: Establishing mechanisms for ongoing monitoring and oversight of control effectiveness, including periodic reviews, testing, and reporting.

"As we roll out these new control systems, it's important to provide training and support to our employees to ensure successful adoption," Michael emphasized, his gaze sweeping across the room. "By fostering a culture of compliance and accountability, we can strengthen our internal controls and safeguard GlobalTech's assets and reputation."

As the team absorbed the details of the implementation plan, a sense of purpose filled the room. They knew that by implementing new control systems effectively, they could enhance GlobalTech's risk management capabilities and ensure the company's continued success in a dynamic and challenging business environment.

With the implementation underway, Michael and his team embarked on a journey of strengthening internal controls, confident in their ability to mitigate risks effectively and safeguard GlobalTech's assets and reputation in an ever-evolving landscape of regulatory requirements and business challenges.

Training Staff on Fraud Prevention and Detection

As GlobalTech fortified its internal control systems, Michael recognized the critical importance of equipping staff with the knowledge and tools to prevent and detect fraud. Understanding that employees are the first line of defense against fraudulent activities, he led his team in developing a comprehensive training program focused on fraud prevention and detection.

In the training room of GlobalTech's headquarters, Michael stood before a group of employees, the room buzzing with anticipation as they prepared to delve into the intricacies of fraud prevention and detection.

"Good morning, everyone," Michael greeted, his voice filled with sincerity. "Today, we're going to discuss fraud prevention and detection to equip you with the knowledge and skills to safeguard GlobalTech's assets and reputation. By fostering a culture of vigilance and integrity, we can protect our company from the damaging effects of fraud."

He began by outlining the objectives of the training program, emphasizing the importance of understanding the red flags of fraud, the consequences of fraudulent behavior, and the role of every employee in maintaining a fraud-free workplace. With clarity and empathy, he explained the impact of fraud on the company's financial health, reputation, and employee morale.

"As we embark on this training, it's crucial that we cultivate a culture of honesty, transparency, and accountability," Michael explained, his tone earnest. "By recognizing the warning signs of fraud and knowing how to report suspicious activities, each of you can play a vital role in protecting GlobalTech's interests and upholding our values."

He then delved into the specifics of the training, covering

topics such as:

1. **Types of Fraud**: Exploring common types of fraud, including financial statement fraud, asset misappropriation, and corruption, and discussing real-life examples to illustrate key concepts.
2. **Red Flags**: Identifying the warning signs of fraudulent behavior, such as unauthorized transactions, unusual accounting entries, and conflicts of interest, and providing guidance on how to respond appropriately.
3. **Reporting Procedures**: Reviewing the company's reporting procedures for suspected fraud, including whistleblower policies, anonymous hotlines, and escalation protocols, and emphasizing the importance of timely and accurate reporting.

"As we conclude this training, I encourage each of you to remain vigilant and proactive in your efforts to prevent and detect fraud," Michael concluded, his gaze sweeping across the room. "By working together and upholding the highest standards of integrity and professionalism, we can safeguard GlobalTech's assets and reputation and ensure our continued success in the years to come."

As the employees absorbed the knowledge imparted during the training, a sense of empowerment filled the room. They knew that by being vigilant and proactive, they could protect GlobalTech from the damaging effects of fraud and contribute to the company's long-term success and sustainability.

With the training program complete, Michael and his team continued their efforts to strengthen internal controls and mitigate risks, confident in their ability to safeguard GlobalTech's assets and reputation in an ever-evolving business landscape.

Ensuring Compliance with Regulatory Requirements

As GlobalTech fortified its internal control systems, Michael understood the paramount importance of ensuring compliance with regulatory requirements. Recognizing that adherence to regulations was essential for maintaining the company's integrity and reputation, he led his team in developing rigorous processes and protocols to ensure compliance across all facets of operations.

In the compliance center of GlobalTech's headquarters, Michael convened his team once more, the atmosphere charged with determination as they prepared to address the intricacies of regulatory compliance.

"Good morning, everyone," Michael greeted, his voice resonating with purpose. "Today, we're going to discuss ensuring compliance with regulatory requirements to uphold GlobalTech's integrity and reputation. By adhering to regulations, we can maintain the trust of our stakeholders and safeguard our company's future."

He began by outlining the objectives of the compliance initiative, emphasizing the importance of understanding and adhering to applicable laws, regulations, and industry standards. With clarity and precision, he explained the role of compliance in mitigating legal and reputational risks, ensuring ethical conduct, and fostering a culture of accountability.

"As we embark on this journey of compliance, it's crucial that we stay informed and proactive in our efforts to meet regulatory requirements," Michael explained, his tone focused. "By establishing robust processes and controls, we can demonstrate our commitment to integrity and ethics in all aspects of our business."

He then delved into the specifics of ensuring compliance, covering topics such as:

1. **Regulatory Landscape**: Providing an overview of relevant laws, regulations, and industry standards that apply to GlobalTech's operations, including financial reporting, data privacy, and environmental regulations.
2. **Compliance Framework**: Developing a comprehensive compliance framework to assess, monitor, and report on compliance with regulatory requirements, including policies, procedures, and controls.
3. **Training and Awareness**: Providing ongoing training and awareness programs to educate employees on their responsibilities and obligations under applicable regulations, and to foster a culture of compliance throughout the organization.

"As we navigate the complexities of regulatory compliance, it's important to cultivate a collaborative approach and engage stakeholders from across the organization," Michael emphasized, his gaze sweeping across the room. "By working together and upholding the highest standards of ethics and integrity, we can ensure that GlobalTech remains a trusted and respected leader in our industry."

As the team absorbed the details of the compliance initiative, a sense of determination filled the room. They knew that by prioritizing compliance and ethics, they could uphold GlobalTech's reputation and credibility, and ensure the company's continued success and sustainability in a highly regulated business environment.

With the compliance initiative underway, Michael and his team continued their efforts to strengthen internal controls, mitigate risks, and safeguard GlobalTech's assets and reputation, confident in their ability to uphold the highest standards of integrity and professionalism in all aspects of their work.

Michael's Role in Fostering a Culture of Accountability

Amidst the efforts to fortify GlobalTech's internal controls, Michael recognized his pivotal role in fostering a culture of accountability throughout the organization. Understanding that leadership sets the tone for ethical behavior and integrity, he dedicated himself to exemplifying and promoting these values at every opportunity.

In the executive suite of GlobalTech's headquarters, Michael gathered his leadership team once more, the air charged with anticipation as they prepared to discuss the importance of accountability in driving organizational success.

"Good morning, everyone," Michael greeted, his voice infused with sincerity. "Today, we're going to delve into the crucial topic of accountability and its role in shaping our company's culture. By fostering a culture of accountability, we can empower our employees to take ownership of their actions, uphold our values, and drive excellence in everything we do."

He began by outlining his vision for a culture of accountability, emphasizing the importance of transparency, integrity, and responsibility in all interactions and decisions. With clarity and conviction, he shared personal anecdotes and insights, illustrating the impact of accountability on individual and organizational performance.

"As leaders, it's our responsibility to set the tone for accountability and integrity within our organization," Michael explained, his tone resolute. "By modeling the behaviors we expect from others and holding ourselves and each other accountable, we can create an environment where trust thrives, and high performance is the norm."

He then delved into the specifics of his role in fostering a culture of accountability, covering topics such as:

1. **Leading by Example**: Demonstrating accountability in his own actions and decisions, and holding himself to the same high standards he expects from others.
2. **Communicating Expectations**: Clearly articulating expectations for accountability and integrity to all employees, and providing ongoing guidance and support to help them meet these expectations.
3. **Recognizing and Rewarding Accountability**: Acknowledging and celebrating instances of accountability and integrity, and reinforcing desired behaviors through recognition programs and incentives.

"As leaders, we have the power to shape the culture of our organization," Michael emphasized, his gaze sweeping across the room. "By fostering a culture of accountability, we can unlock the full potential of our employees, drive innovation and collaboration, and achieve our shared goals."

As the leadership team absorbed Michael's words, a sense of determination filled the room. They knew that by embracing accountability and integrity in their own actions and decisions, they could inspire others to do the same, and create a workplace where excellence flourished, and trust abounded.

With Michael leading the charge, GlobalTech embarked on a journey of cultural transformation, confident in their ability to foster a culture of accountability, integrity, and excellence, and ensure the company's continued success and sustainability in a rapidly evolving business landscape.

10

Chapter 10: Decision-Making Excellence

Applying Relevant Costing to Real-Life Scenarios

As GlobalTech aimed to achieve decision-making excellence, Michael recognized the critical importance of applying relevant costing principles to real-life scenarios. Understanding that informed decision-making relied on accurate and insightful cost analysis, he led his team in exploring practical applications of relevant costing to drive strategic and operational decisions.

In the innovation hub of GlobalTech's headquarters, Michael convened his team once more, the atmosphere buzzing with anticipation as they prepared to delve into the intricacies of relevant costing.

"Good morning, everyone," Michael greeted, his voice filled with enthusiasm. "Today, we're going to explore the application of relevant costing to real-life scenarios to drive informed decision-making for GlobalTech. By understanding the true costs and benefits of our options, we can make strategic and operational decisions that maximize value for our company."

He began by outlining the objectives of the session, emphasizing the importance of relevant costing in evaluating alternative courses of action, assessing profitability, and optimizing resource allocation. With clarity and precision, he explained the principles of relevant costing, including the identification of relevant costs and benefits, the consideration of opportunity costs, and the analysis of incremental effects.

"As we apply relevant costing to real-life scenarios, it's crucial that we consider both quantitative and qualitative factors," Michael explained, his tone focused. "By taking a holistic approach to decision-making, we can ensure that our choices align with our strategic objectives and contribute to the long-term success of our company."

He then delved into the specifics of the application, presenting a series of case studies and examples to illustrate the principles of relevant costing in action. From pricing decisions and product mix optimization to make-or-buy analysis and capital investment evaluation, each scenario provided valuable insights into the power of relevant costing to inform and guide decision-making.

"As we navigate the complexities of decision-making, it's important to remember that relevant costing is not just about numbers," Michael emphasized, his gaze sweeping across the room. "It's about understanding the underlying drivers of costs and benefits, and using that knowledge to make informed and strategic choices that create value for our company."

As the team absorbed the insights shared during the session, a sense of empowerment filled the room. They knew that by applying relevant costing principles to real-life scenarios, they could make decisions with confidence, clarity, and impact, driving GlobalTech's success and sustainability in a dynamic and competitive business environment.

With the session concluded, Michael and his team continued their journey of decision-making excellence, armed with the knowledge and tools to leverage relevant costing effectively and drive value for GlobalTech in the years to come.

Utilizing Cost-Volume-Profit Analysis for Strategic Decisions

As GlobalTech aimed to achieve decision-making excellence, Michael delved into the strategic application of cost-volume-profit (CVP) analysis. Recognizing the pivotal role of CVP analysis in evaluating the relationship between costs, volume, and profits, he led his team in exploring how this powerful tool could inform strategic decisions and drive long-term success for the company.

In the boardroom of GlobalTech's headquarters, Michael convened his team once again, the atmosphere charged with anticipation as they prepared to unlock the insights of CVP analysis.

"Good morning, everyone," Michael greeted, his voice resonating with determination. "Today, we're going to explore the strategic application of cost-volume-profit analysis to drive informed decision-making for GlobalTech. By understanding the interplay between costs, volume, and profits, we can make strategic choices that maximize our company's profitability and sustainability."

He began by outlining the objectives of the session, emphasizing the importance of CVP analysis in assessing the impact of various factors on the company's financial performance, such as changes in sales volume, pricing strategies, and cost structures. With clarity and precision, he explained the key components of CVP analysis, including contribution margin, breakeven point, and margin of safety.

"As we delve into the strategic application of CVP analysis, it's crucial that we consider both short-term and long-term implications," Michael explained, his tone focused. "By using CVP analysis to evaluate different scenarios and alternative courses of action, we can identify opportunities for growth, optimize resource allocation, and mitigate risks effectively."

He then delved into the specifics of the application, presenting a series of strategic scenarios and examples to illustrate the insights that CVP analysis could provide. From pricing decisions and product mix optimization to sales forecasting and budgeting, each scenario showcased the power of CVP analysis to inform strategic decision-making and drive value creation.

"As we navigate the complexities of strategic decision-making, it's important to leverage CVP analysis as a strategic tool," Michael emphasized, his gaze sweeping across the room. "By understanding the relationship between costs, volume, and profits, we can make decisions that not only maximize short-term profitability but also position GlobalTech for long-term success and sustainability."

As the team absorbed the insights shared during the session, a sense of empowerment filled the room. They knew that by utilizing CVP analysis for strategic decisions, they could make informed choices that aligned with GlobalTech's strategic objectives and contributed to the company's growth and profitability in the years to come.

With the session concluded, Michael and his team continued their journey of decision-making excellence, armed with the knowledge and tools to leverage CVP analysis effectively and drive value for GlobalTech in an increasingly complex and competitive business landscape.

Make or Buy Decisions: A Case Study

In the pursuit of decision-making excellence, Michael delved into the intricate realm of make or buy decisions, using a compelling case study to illuminate the strategic considerations involved. Recognizing the significance of these decisions in optimizing resource allocation and enhancing competitiveness, he led his team in dissecting a real-world scenario to uncover insights and inform future strategic choices for GlobalTech.

In the collaboration room of GlobalTech's headquarters, Michael gathered his team once more, the atmosphere tinged with anticipation as they prepared to unravel the complexities of make or buy decisions.

"Good morning, everyone," Michael greeted, his voice charged with enthusiasm. "Today, we're going to delve into the strategic implications of make or buy decisions through a captivating case study. By understanding the trade-offs and considerations involved, we can make informed choices that maximize value for GlobalTech."

He began by setting the stage, introducing the case study—a dilemma faced by GlobalTech's procurement department regarding the production of a critical component for its flagship product. With clarity and precision, he outlined the key factors to be considered, including production costs, quality control, supply chain reliability, and strategic alignment.

"As we immerse ourselves in this case study, it's essential to weigh the pros and cons of making the component in-house versus outsourcing it to a third-party supplier," Michael explained, his tone focused. "By conducting a thorough analysis of the relevant factors, we can determine the most advantageous course of action for GlobalTech."

He then guided his team through the intricacies of the decision-making process, encouraging active participation and critical thinking. From cost comparisons and risk assessments to capacity constraints and strategic implications, each aspect of the case study offered valuable insights into the complexity of make or buy decisions in a real-world context.

"As we evaluate the options before us, it's important to consider not only short-term cost savings but also long-term strategic implications," Michael emphasized, his gaze sweeping across the room. "By making a well-informed decision, we can position GlobalTech for sustained success and competitiveness in the marketplace."

As the team immersed themselves in the case study, a palpable sense of engagement filled the room. They knew that by grappling with the complexities of make or buy decisions, they could sharpen their analytical skills and contribute to the strategic direction of GlobalTech.

With the case study discussion concluded, Michael and his team continued their pursuit of decision-making excellence, armed with the insights and perspectives gained from the session. They were determined to apply their newfound knowledge to future challenges and opportunities, driving value creation and innovation for GlobalTech in an ever-evolving business landscape.

Evaluating Outsourcing Opportunities

As GlobalTech sought to excel in decision-making, Michael led his team into the realm of evaluating outsourcing opportunities. Recognizing the potential benefits and risks associated with outsourcing, he guided his team in dissecting various scenarios to determine the strategic implications and optimize resource allocation for GlobalTech.

In the strategy room of GlobalTech's headquarters, Michael convened his team once again, the atmosphere charged with anticipation as they delved into the intricacies of evaluating outsourcing opportunities.

"Good morning, everyone," Michael greeted, his voice filled with determination. "Today, we're going to explore the strategic implications of outsourcing through a series of compelling scenarios. By understanding the trade-offs involved, we can make informed decisions that enhance GlobalTech's competitiveness and profitability."

He began by setting the stage, introducing a range of outsourcing opportunities across different functions, including manufacturing, IT services, and customer support. With clarity and precision, he outlined the key factors to consider, such as cost savings, quality control, operational flexibility, and strategic alignment.

"As we assess these outsourcing opportunities, it's essential to conduct a comprehensive analysis of the potential benefits and risks," Michael explained, his tone focused. "By weighing the short-term cost savings against the long-term strategic implications, we can determine the optimal approach for GlobalTech."

He then guided his team through the evaluation process,

encouraging critical thinking and collaboration. From cost comparisons and risk assessments to vendor selection and contract negotiations, each scenario offered valuable insights into the complexities of outsourcing decisions in a dynamic business environment.

"As we navigate the complexities of outsourcing, it's important to remain vigilant and proactive in managing risks and safeguarding GlobalTech's interests," Michael emphasized, his gaze sweeping across the room. "By making well-informed outsourcing decisions, we can enhance our operational efficiency, drive innovation, and focus our resources on core competencies that deliver the greatest value to our company."

As the team delved deeper into the evaluation process, a sense of purpose filled the room. They knew that by rigorously assessing outsourcing opportunities, they could unlock new avenues for growth and competitiveness, positioning GlobalTech as a leader in its industry.

With the evaluation concluded, Michael and his team continued their journey of decision-making excellence, armed with the insights and perspectives gained from the session. They were determined to leverage outsourcing strategically to drive value creation and innovation for GlobalTech in an increasingly competitive global marketplace.

Pricing Decisions Based on Management Accounting Data

In the quest for decision-making excellence, Michael turned his attention to the strategic realm of pricing decisions, leveraging management accounting data to inform and optimize pricing strategies for GlobalTech's products and services. Recognizing the pivotal role of pricing in revenue generation and market positioning, he guided his team in dissecting pricing scenarios to unlock insights and drive profitability for the company.

In the innovation lab of GlobalTech's headquarters, Michael convened his team once more, the air buzzing with anticipation as they prepared to explore the nuances of pricing decisions.

"Good morning, everyone," Michael greeted, his voice brimming with enthusiasm. "Today, we're going to delve into the strategic implications of pricing decisions based on management accounting data. By leveraging insights from our accounting systems, we can develop pricing strategies that maximize value for GlobalTech and enhance our competitive advantage in the marketplace."

He began by framing the discussion, highlighting the importance of aligning pricing decisions with GlobalTech's strategic objectives and market dynamics. With clarity and precision, he outlined the key factors to consider, such as product costs, customer value perceptions, competitive landscape, and pricing elasticity.

"As we analyze pricing scenarios, it's crucial to leverage management accounting data to understand the true costs and profitability of our products and services," Michael explained, his tone focused. "By incorporating insights from our accounting systems, we can set prices that not only cover our costs but also capture the value we deliver to customers and drive sustainable growth for GlobalTech."

He then guided his team through a series of pricing scenarios, encouraging critical thinking and collaboration. From cost-plus pricing and value-based pricing to dynamic pricing strategies, each scenario offered valuable insights into the complexities of pricing decisions in a dynamic business environment.

"As we navigate the complexities of pricing decisions, it's important to strike a balance between profitability and market competitiveness," Michael emphasized, his gaze sweeping across the room. "By leveraging management accounting data to inform our pricing strategies, we can ensure that GlobalTech remains a leader in its industry and delivers value to both customers and shareholders."

As the team delved deeper into the analysis, a sense of determination filled the room. They knew that by leveraging management accounting data to inform pricing decisions, they could unlock new opportunities for revenue growth and profitability, positioning GlobalTech as a leader in its industry.

With the discussion concluded, Michael and his team continued their pursuit of decision-making excellence, armed with the insights and perspectives gained from the session. They were determined to apply their newfound knowledge to pricing decisions and drive sustainable growth and competitiveness for GlobalTech in an ever-evolving business landscape.

Using Decision Trees to Map Out Possible Outcomes

In the pursuit of decision-making excellence, Michael introduced his team to the strategic tool of decision trees, harnessing its power to map out possible outcomes and inform strategic choices for GlobalTech. Recognizing the complexity of decision-making in a dynamic business environment, he guided his team in constructing decision trees to visualize and analyze various scenarios, enabling them to make informed and strategic decisions for the company's success.

In the strategy room of GlobalTech's headquarters, Michael gathered his team once more, the atmosphere charged with anticipation as they prepared to explore the intricacies of decision trees.

"Good morning, everyone," Michael greeted, his voice filled with determination. "Today, we're going to delve into the strategic implications of using decision trees to map out possible outcomes for GlobalTech. By visualizing different scenarios and their probabilities, we can make informed decisions that maximize value and mitigate risks for our company."

He began by framing the discussion, explaining the concept of decision trees and their relevance in evaluating complex decisions with uncertain outcomes. With clarity and precision, he outlined the key components of decision trees, including decision nodes, chance nodes, and outcome nodes, and their role in visualizing decision options and their potential consequences.

"As we construct decision trees, it's essential to consider both quantitative data and qualitative insights," Michael explained, his tone focused. "By mapping out possible outcomes and their probabilities, we can assess the risks and rewards associated with different decision options and identify the optimal path forward for GlobalTech."

He then guided his team through the construction of decision trees for various strategic decisions, encouraging critical thinking and collaboration. From product development strategies and market expansion initiatives to investment decisions and risk management strategies, each decision tree offered valuable insights into the complexities of decision-making in a dynamic and uncertain business environment.

"As we navigate the complexities of decision-making, it's important to leverage decision trees as a strategic tool," Michael emphasized, his gaze sweeping across the room. "By visualizing possible outcomes and their probabilities, we can make decisions that not only maximize our chances of success but also prepare us to effectively manage risks and uncertainties in our business."

As the team immersed themselves in constructing decision trees, a sense of empowerment filled the room. They knew that by visualizing and analyzing different scenarios, they could make informed and strategic decisions that aligned with GlobalTech's strategic objectives and contributed to the company's long-term success and sustainability.

With the session concluded, Michael and his team continued their journey of decision-making excellence, armed with the insights and perspectives gained from the exploration of decision trees. They were determined to apply their newfound knowledge to future challenges and opportunities, driving value creation and innovation for GlobalTech in an increasingly complex and uncertain business landscape.

11

Chapter 11: Cost Management Innovations

Differentiating Between Cost Control and Cost Reduction

In the realm of cost management innovations, Michael delved into the crucial distinction between cost control and cost reduction, illuminating their significance in driving efficiency and profitability for GlobalTech. Recognizing the nuanced approach required to optimize costs while maintaining operational effectiveness, he guided his team in exploring strategies to differentiate between these concepts and implement them effectively in the company's operations.

In the strategy room of GlobalTech's headquarters, Michael gathered his team once again, the atmosphere charged with anticipation as they prepared to unravel the complexities of cost management innovations.

"Good morning, everyone," Michael greeted, his voice resonating with purpose. "Today, we're going to delve into the strategic implications of differentiating between cost control and cost reduction for GlobalTech. By understanding the nuances of these concepts, we can implement strategies that optimize costs while preserving our ability to deliver value to our customers and stakeholders."

He began by framing the discussion, explaining the fundamental differences between cost control and cost reduction and their respective roles in cost management. With clarity and precision, he outlined the key components of each concept, emphasizing their strategic implications and the importance of striking a balance between them.

"As we explore cost management innovations, it's essential to recognize that cost control focuses on managing costs within predetermined targets, while cost reduction aims to lower costs through various initiatives," Michael explained, his tone focused. "By understanding the differences between these concepts, we can develop strategies that optimize costs without sacrificing quality or performance."

He then guided his team through a series of case studies and examples to illustrate the practical application of cost control and cost reduction strategies in real-world scenarios. From process improvements and efficiency enhancements to supplier negotiations and technology investments, each example offered valuable insights into the nuances of cost management and the strategic decisions required to achieve sustainable cost optimization.

"As we navigate the complexities of cost management, it's important to adopt a holistic approach that balances cost control and cost reduction initiatives," Michael emphasized, his gaze sweeping across the room. "By implementing innovative strategies that optimize costs while preserving value, we can position GlobalTech for long-term success and competitiveness in the marketplace."

As the team absorbed the insights shared during the discussion, a sense of clarity filled the room. They knew that by differentiating between cost control and cost reduction and implementing innovative strategies accordingly, they could drive efficiency, profitability, and sustainability for GlobalTech in an increasingly competitive business landscape.

With the discussion concluded, Michael and his team continued their journey of cost management innovations, armed with the knowledge and perspectives gained from the exploration of cost control and cost reduction strategies. They were determined to apply their newfound understanding to optimize costs and drive value creation for GlobalTech in the years to come.

Implementing Value Engineering Projects

In the pursuit of cost management innovations, Michael turned his focus towards implementing value engineering projects, recognizing their potential to drive efficiency and enhance value for GlobalTech. Understanding the importance of maximizing value while minimizing costs, he guided his team in exploring strategies to implement value engineering projects effectively and achieve sustainable cost optimization.

In the project room of GlobalTech's headquarters, Michael gathered his team once again, the atmosphere buzzing with anticipation as they prepared to delve into the realm of value engineering.

"Good morning, everyone," Michael greeted, his voice filled with determination. "Today, we're going to explore the strategic implications of implementing value engineering projects for GlobalTech. By optimizing value while minimizing costs, we can drive efficiency and enhance competitiveness in the marketplace."

He began by framing the discussion, explaining the concept of value engineering and its role in identifying opportunities to improve the value of products and processes while reducing costs. With clarity and precision, he outlined the key principles of value engineering, emphasizing the importance of collaboration, creativity, and continuous improvement.

"As we embark on value engineering projects, it's essential to adopt a systematic approach that involves cross-functional teams and fosters innovation," Michael explained, his tone focused. "By leveraging the collective expertise of our team members and challenging conventional thinking, we can uncover opportunities to optimize value and drive cost savings for GlobalTech."

He then guided his team through a series of case studies and examples to illustrate the practical application of value engineering in real-world scenarios. From product redesigns and process improvements to supply chain optimizations and technology upgrades, each example offered valuable insights into the potential impact of value engineering on GlobalTech's operations and bottom line.

"As we implement value engineering projects, it's important to prioritize initiatives that deliver the greatest value to our customers and stakeholders," Michael emphasized, his gaze sweeping across the room. "By focusing on innovation and efficiency, we can position GlobalTech as a leader in its industry and drive sustainable growth and profitability."

As the team absorbed the insights shared during the discussion, a sense of enthusiasm filled the room. They knew that by embracing value engineering and implementing projects effectively, they could unlock new opportunities for cost optimization and value creation for GlobalTech.

With the discussion concluded, Michael and his team continued their journey of cost management innovations, armed with the knowledge and perspectives gained from the exploration of value engineering projects. They were determined to apply their newfound understanding to drive efficiency, enhance value, and achieve sustainable cost optimization for GlobalTech in the years to come.

Introducing Kaizen Costing for Continuous Improvement

In the pursuit of cost management innovations, Michael introduced the concept of Kaizen Costing, recognizing its potential to foster a culture of continuous improvement and drive efficiency for GlobalTech. Understanding the importance of incremental enhancements in optimizing costs, he guided his team in exploring strategies to implement Kaizen Costing effectively and instill a mindset of continuous improvement throughout the organization.

In the conference room of GlobalTech's headquarters, Michael gathered his team once more, the air filled with anticipation as they prepared to delve into the principles of Kaizen Costing.

"Good morning, everyone," Michael greeted, his voice filled with enthusiasm. "Today, we're going to explore the strategic implications of introducing Kaizen Costing for GlobalTech. By embracing a culture of continuous improvement, we can drive efficiency and enhance our competitive advantage in the marketplace."

He began by framing the discussion, explaining the concept of Kaizen Costing and its emphasis on incremental improvements in cost management processes. With clarity and precision, he outlined the key principles of Kaizen, including teamwork, employee empowerment, and a focus on waste reduction.

"As we embark on our Kaizen journey, it's essential to foster a culture of continuous improvement that empowers all employees to identify and implement cost-saving opportunities," Michael explained, his tone focused. "By embracing Kaizen Costing, we can unlock the full potential of our workforce and drive sustainable cost reductions for GlobalTech."

He then guided his team through a series of case studies and examples to illustrate the practical application of Kaizen Costing in real-world scenarios. From process streamlining and standardization to employee training and supplier collaboration, each example showcased the transformative impact of Kaizen on cost management and operational efficiency.

"As we introduce Kaizen Costing, it's important to prioritize initiatives that deliver measurable results and align with our strategic objectives," Michael emphasized, his gaze sweeping across the room. "By fostering a culture of continuous improvement, we can drive innovation, optimize costs, and achieve excellence in everything we do."

As the team absorbed the insights shared during the discussion, a sense of empowerment filled the room. They knew that by embracing Kaizen Costing and committing to continuous improvement, they could unlock new opportunities for efficiency and excellence for GlobalTech.

With the discussion concluded, Michael and his team continued their journey of cost management innovations, armed with the knowledge and perspectives gained from the exploration of Kaizen Costing. They were determined to apply their newfound understanding to drive continuous improvement and achieve sustainable cost optimization for GlobalTech in the years to come.

Applying Activity-Based Management Principles

In the pursuit of cost management innovations, Michael turned his attention towards the application of Activity-Based Management (ABM) principles, recognizing their potential to drive efficiency and strategic decision-making for GlobalTech. Understanding the importance of aligning costs with activities and value creation, he guided his team in exploring strategies to implement ABM effectively and optimize performance across the organization.

In the boardroom of GlobalTech's headquarters, Michael convened his team once more, the atmosphere charged with anticipation as they prepared to delve into the principles of Activity-Based Management.

"Good morning, everyone," Michael greeted, his voice resonating with purpose. "Today, we're going to explore the strategic implications of applying Activity-Based Management principles for GlobalTech. By aligning costs with activities and value creation, we can drive efficiency and enhance our competitiveness in the marketplace."

He began by framing the discussion, explaining the concept of Activity-Based Management and its focus on understanding and managing the activities that drive costs within an organization. With clarity and precision, he outlined the key principles of ABM, including activity analysis, cost allocation, and performance measurement.

"As we implement Activity-Based Management, it's essential to adopt a systematic approach that identifies and prioritizes value-added activities," Michael explained, his tone focused. "By aligning costs with activities and understanding their contribution to value creation, we can make informed decisions that optimize performance and drive sustainable growth for GlobalTech."

He then guided his team through a series of case studies and examples to illustrate the practical application of ABM in real-world scenarios. From product costing and customer profitability analysis to process optimization and resource allocation, each example showcased the transformative impact of ABM on cost management and strategic decision-making.

"As we apply Activity-Based Management principles, it's important to leverage technology and data analytics to gain insights into our operations and drive continuous improvement," Michael emphasized, his gaze sweeping across the room. "By aligning costs with activities and focusing on value creation, we can optimize performance and achieve excellence in everything we do."

As the team absorbed the insights shared during the discussion, a sense of determination filled the room. They knew that by embracing Activity-Based Management and committing to aligning costs with value creation, they could unlock new opportunities for efficiency and strategic success for GlobalTech.

With the discussion concluded, Michael and his team continued their journey of cost management innovations, armed with the knowledge and perspectives gained from the exploration of ABM principles. They were determined to apply their newfound understanding to drive performance optimization and achieve sustainable cost management for GlobalTech in the years to come.

Setting Target Costing for New Product Development

In the realm of cost management innovations, Michael turned his focus towards setting target costing for new product development, recognizing its pivotal role in driving efficiency and profitability for GlobalTech's future endeavors. Understanding the importance of aligning costs with market demands and strategic objectives, he guided his team in exploring strategies to implement target costing effectively and ensure the success of new product launches.

In the innovation lab of GlobalTech's headquarters, Michael gathered his team once more, the air buzzing with anticipation as they prepared to delve into the principles of target costing.

"Good morning, everyone," Michael greeted, his voice filled with determination. "Today, we're going to explore the strategic implications of setting target costing for new product development at GlobalTech. By aligning costs with market expectations and strategic objectives, we can drive efficiency and enhance our competitiveness in the marketplace."

He began by framing the discussion, explaining the concept of target costing and its importance in designing products that meet customer needs while achieving profitability targets. With clarity and precision, he outlined the key components of target costing, including market analysis, cost estimation, and cost reduction strategies.

"As we embark on new product development initiatives, it's essential to adopt a customer-centric approach that focuses on delivering value at an affordable price," Michael explained, his tone focused. "By setting target costs based on market expectations and competitive benchmarks, we can ensure the success of our new products and drive sustainable growth for GlobalTech."

He then guided his team through a series of case studies and examples to illustrate the practical application of target costing in real-world scenarios. From product design and feature prioritization to supplier negotiations and cost optimization, each example showcased the transformative impact of target costing on new product development and profitability.

"As we set target costing for new product development, it's important to collaborate closely with cross-functional teams and leverage insights from market research and customer feedback," Michael emphasized, his gaze sweeping across the room. "By aligning costs with customer value and strategic objectives, we can create innovative products that resonate with our target market and drive long-term success for GlobalTech."

As the team absorbed the insights shared during the discussion, a sense of excitement filled the room. They knew that by embracing target costing and committing to aligning costs with market demands, they could unlock new opportunities for innovation and strategic success for GlobalTech.

With the discussion concluded, Michael and his team continued their journey of cost management innovations, armed with the knowledge and perspectives gained from the exploration of target costing principles. They were determined to apply their newfound understanding to drive efficiency, enhance value, and achieve sustainable growth for GlobalTech in the years to come.

Life-cycle Costing to Manage Costs Over Product Lifespan

In the quest for cost management innovations, Michael directed his focus towards the strategic application of life-cycle costing, recognizing its significance in managing costs over the entire lifespan of a product. Understanding the importance of considering not only the upfront costs but also the long-term implications, he guided his team in exploring strategies to implement life-cycle costing effectively and ensure the sustainability of GlobalTech's products in the marketplace.

In the strategic planning room of GlobalTech's headquarters, Michael gathered his team once more, the atmosphere charged with anticipation as they prepared to delve into the principles of life-cycle costing.

"Good morning, everyone," Michael greeted, his voice filled with purpose. "Today, we're going to explore the strategic implications of implementing life-cycle costing for GlobalTech. By considering costs over the entire lifespan of our products, we can make informed decisions that drive efficiency and enhance our competitiveness in the marketplace."

He began by framing the discussion, explaining the concept of life-cycle costing and its importance in evaluating costs from product conception to disposal. With clarity and precision, he outlined the key components of life-cycle costing, including acquisition costs, operating costs, maintenance costs, and disposal costs.

"As we assess the costs associated with our products, it's essential to adopt a holistic approach that considers not only the upfront costs but also the long-term implications," Michael explained, his tone focused. "By implementing life-cycle costing, we can identify cost-saving opportunities and make strategic decisions that optimize costs over the entire lifespan of our products."

He then guided his team through a series of case studies and examples to illustrate the practical application of life-cycle costing in real-world scenarios. From product design and material selection to manufacturing processes and end-of-life disposal, each example showcased the transformative impact of life-cycle costing on cost management and strategic decision-making.

"As we implement life-cycle costing, it's important to collaborate closely with suppliers, customers, and other stakeholders to identify opportunities for cost optimization at every stage of the product lifecycle," Michael emphasized, his gaze sweeping across the room. "By considering costs comprehensively, we can create products that deliver value to our customers and drive sustainable growth for GlobalTech."

As the team absorbed the insights shared during the discussion, a sense of determination filled the room. They knew that by embracing life-cycle costing and committing to considering costs over the entire product lifespan, they could unlock new opportunities for efficiency and strategic success for GlobalTech.

With the discussion concluded, Michael and his team continued their journey of cost management innovations, armed with the knowledge and perspectives gained from the exploration of life-cycle costing principles. They were determined to apply their newfound understanding to drive efficiency, enhance value, and achieve sustainable growth for GlobalTech in the years to come.

12

Chapter 12: Financial Planning and Analysis

The Strategic Role of FP&A in the Corporation

As the journey through financial management continued, Michael directed his focus towards Financial Planning and Analysis (FP&A), recognizing its pivotal role in shaping the strategic direction of GlobalTech. Understanding the importance of aligning financial goals with strategic objectives, he gathered his team to explore the strategic significance of FP&A in driving decision-making and enhancing financial performance.

In the boardroom of GlobalTech's headquarters, Michael convened his team once more, the air filled with anticipation as they prepared to delve into the realm of FP&A.

"Good morning, everyone," Michael greeted, his voice filled with determination. "Today, we're going to explore the strategic role of Financial Planning and Analysis in driving the success of GlobalTech. By aligning financial goals with our strategic objectives, we can make informed decisions that drive efficiency and enhance our competitiveness in the marketplace."

He began by framing the discussion, explaining the concept of FP&A and its importance in providing insights and guidance for strategic decision-making. With clarity and precision, he outlined the key components of FP&A, including budgeting, forecasting, variance analysis, and strategic planning.

"As we embark on our FP&A journey, it's essential to adopt a forward-looking approach that anticipates opportunities and challenges," Michael explained, his tone focused. "By leveraging financial data and analysis, we can develop actionable insights that inform strategic decisions and drive sustainable growth for GlobalTech."

He then guided his team through a series of case studies and examples to illustrate the strategic significance of FP&A in real-world scenarios. From financial forecasting and scenario analysis to investment evaluation and resource allocation, each example showcased the transformative impact of FP&A on strategic decision-making and financial performance.

"As we embrace FP&A, it's important to foster collaboration and communication across departments and functions," Michael emphasized, his gaze sweeping across the room. "By aligning financial goals with strategic objectives and fostering a culture of continuous improvement, we can drive efficiency, enhance value, and achieve excellence in everything we do."

As the team absorbed the insights shared during the discussion, a sense of excitement filled the room. They knew that by embracing the strategic role of FP&A and committing to aligning financial goals with strategic objectives, they could unlock new opportunities for success and growth for

GlobalTech.

With the discussion concluded, Michael and his team continued their journey of financial planning and analysis, armed with the knowledge and perspectives gained from the exploration of FP&A principles. They were determined to apply their newfound understanding to drive strategic decision-making and enhance financial performance for GlobalTech in the years to come.

Integrating Budgeting and Forecasting with Strategic Planning

As the exploration of Financial Planning and Analysis (FP&A) continued, Michael directed his attention towards the strategic integration of budgeting and forecasting with strategic planning, recognizing its pivotal role in aligning financial goals with the long-term objectives of GlobalTech. Understanding the importance of a cohesive approach to financial management, he gathered his team to explore strategies for integrating budgeting and forecasting seamlessly into the strategic planning process.

In the strategy room of GlobalTech's headquarters, Michael convened his team once more, the atmosphere charged with anticipation as they prepared to delve into the integration of budgeting and forecasting with strategic planning.

"Good morning, everyone," Michael greeted, his voice filled with purpose. "Today, we're going to explore the strategic implications of integrating budgeting and forecasting with strategic planning at GlobalTech. By aligning our financial goals with our strategic objectives, we can make informed decisions that drive efficiency and enhance our competitiveness in the marketplace."

He began by framing the discussion, explaining the importance of aligning budgeting and forecasting activities with the strategic planning process. With clarity and precision, he outlined the key components of budgeting, forecasting, and strategic planning, emphasizing their interconnectedness and the need for alignment to drive organizational success.

"As we integrate budgeting and forecasting with strategic planning, it's essential to adopt a holistic approach that considers both short-term financial targets and long-term strategic objectives," Michael explained, his tone focused. "By leveraging budgeting and forecasting as strategic tools, we can develop actionable plans that drive sustainable growth and value creation for GlobalTech."

He then guided his team through a series of case studies and examples to illustrate the strategic integration of budgeting and forecasting with strategic planning in real-world scenarios. From scenario analysis and sensitivity testing to resource allocation and performance measurement, each example showcased the transformative impact of aligning financial goals with strategic objectives.

"As we embrace the integration of budgeting and forecasting with strategic planning, it's important to foster collaboration and communication across departments and functions," Michael emphasized, his gaze sweeping across the room. "By aligning our financial plans with our strategic vision, we can navigate uncertainties and capitalize on opportunities to achieve excellence in everything we do."

As the team absorbed the insights shared during the discussion, a sense of determination filled the room. They knew that by integrating budgeting and forecasting with strategic planning and committing to alignment with the company's long-term objectives, they could unlock new opportunities for success and growth for GlobalTech.

With the discussion concluded, Michael and his team continued their journey of financial planning and analysis, armed with the knowledge and perspectives gained from the exploration of integrated budgeting and forecasting principles. They were determined to apply their newfound understanding to drive strategic decision-making and enhance financial performance for GlobalTech in the years to come.

Conducting Variance Analysis to Guide Financial Decisions

In the realm of Financial Planning and Analysis (FP&A), Michael turned his focus towards conducting variance analysis, recognizing its critical role in guiding financial decisions and ensuring the success of GlobalTech's strategic initiatives. Understanding the importance of identifying and understanding deviations from planned outcomes, he gathered his team to explore the strategic significance of variance analysis in driving performance improvement and enhancing financial management.

In the conference room of GlobalTech's headquarters, Michael convened his team once more, the atmosphere buzzing with anticipation as they prepared to delve into the principles of variance analysis.

"Good morning, everyone," Michael greeted, his voice filled with purpose. "Today, we're going to explore the strategic implications of conducting variance analysis for GlobalTech. By identifying and understanding deviations from planned outcomes, we can make informed decisions that drive performance improvement and enhance our competitiveness in the marketplace."

He began by framing the discussion, explaining the concept of variance analysis and its importance in evaluating performance against targets. With clarity and precision, he outlined the key components of variance analysis, including identifying variances, investigating their causes, and taking corrective actions.

"As we conduct variance analysis, it's essential to adopt a proactive approach that addresses deviations from planned outcomes in a timely manner," Michael explained, his tone focused. "By leveraging variance analysis as a strategic tool, we can identify areas for improvement and take corrective actions to ensure the success of our strategic initiatives."

He then guided his team through a series of case studies and examples to illustrate the practical application of variance analysis in real-world scenarios. From budget variances and revenue shortfalls to cost overruns and efficiency gains, each example showcased the transformative impact of variance analysis on performance management and decision-making.

"As we embrace variance analysis, it's important to foster a culture of accountability and continuous improvement," Michael emphasized, his gaze sweeping across the room. "By empowering our teams to identify and address variances, we can drive performance improvement and achieve excellence in everything we do."

As the team absorbed the insights shared during the discussion, a sense of empowerment filled the room. They knew that by conducting variance analysis and committing to proactive performance management, they could unlock new opportunities for success and growth for GlobalTech.

With the discussion concluded, Michael and his team continued their journey of financial planning and analysis, armed with the knowledge and perspectives gained from the exploration of variance analysis principles. They were determined to apply their newfound understanding to drive performance improvement and enhance financial management for GlobalTech in the years to come.

Scenario and Sensitivity Analysis for Risk Management

As the exploration of Financial Planning and Analysis (FP&A) progressed, Michael directed his attention towards scenario and sensitivity analysis, recognizing their pivotal role in risk management and strategic decision-making for GlobalTech. Understanding the importance of anticipating and mitigating potential risks, he gathered his team to explore strategies for conducting scenario and sensitivity analysis effectively to safeguard the company's financial health.

In the strategy room of GlobalTech's headquarters, Michael convened his team once more, the air charged with anticipation as they prepared to delve into the principles of scenario and sensitivity analysis.

"Good morning, everyone," Michael greeted, his voice filled with purpose. "Today, we're going to explore the strategic implications of conducting scenario and sensitivity analysis for GlobalTech. By anticipating and mitigating potential risks, we can make informed decisions that safeguard our financial health and enhance our competitiveness in the marketplace."

He began by framing the discussion, explaining the concepts of scenario and sensitivity analysis and their importance in evaluating the impact of various factors on financial outcomes. With clarity and precision, he outlined the key components of scenario and sensitivity analysis, including identifying key variables, constructing scenarios, and assessing their potential impact.

"As we conduct scenario and sensitivity analysis, it's essential to adopt a forward-looking approach that considers different possible outcomes and their likelihood," Michael explained, his tone focused. "By leveraging scenario and sensitivity analysis as strategic tools, we can identify risks and opportunities and develop contingency plans to navigate uncertainties effectively."

He then guided his team through a series of case studies and examples to illustrate the practical application of scenario and sensitivity analysis in real-world scenarios. From market fluctuations and economic downturns to changes in customer preferences and supply chain disruptions, each example showcased the transformative impact of scenario and sensitivity analysis on risk management and decision-making.

"As we embrace scenario and sensitivity analysis, it's important to foster collaboration and communication across departments and functions," Michael emphasized, his gaze sweeping across the room. "By anticipating risks and opportunities and developing proactive strategies, we can enhance our resilience and drive sustainable growth for GlobalTech."

As the team absorbed the insights shared during the discussion, a sense of preparedness filled the room. They knew that by conducting scenario and sensitivity analysis and committing to proactive risk management, they could safeguard GlobalTech's financial health and position the company for long-term success.

With the discussion concluded, Michael and his team continued their journey of financial planning and analysis, armed with the knowledge and perspectives gained from the exploration of scenario and sensitivity analysis principles. They were determined to apply their newfound understanding to navigate uncertainties effectively and drive sustainable growth for GlobalTech in the years to come.

Building Financial Models to Predict Future Outcomes

As the journey through Financial Planning and Analysis (FP&A) unfolded, Michael turned his attention towards building financial models, recognizing their crucial role in predicting future outcomes and informing strategic decision-making for GlobalTech. Understanding the importance of leveraging data and analytics to forecast financial performance, he gathered his team to explore strategies for constructing robust financial models that would guide the company's future endeavors.

In the analytics hub of GlobalTech's headquarters, Michael convened his team once more, the atmosphere charged with anticipation as they prepared to delve into the intricacies of building financial models.

"Good morning, everyone," Michael greeted, his voice brimming with enthusiasm. "Today, we're going to explore the strategic implications of building financial models for GlobalTech. By leveraging data and analytics to forecast future outcomes, we can make informed decisions that drive efficiency and enhance our competitiveness in the marketplace."

He began by framing the discussion, explaining the importance of building financial models and their role in providing insights into potential financial scenarios. With clarity and precision, he outlined the key components of financial modeling, including data collection, model development, and scenario analysis.

"As we build financial models, it's essential to adopt a rigorous approach that incorporates relevant data and assumptions," Michael explained, his tone focused. "By leveraging financial models as strategic tools, we can anticipate future outcomes and develop strategies to capitalize on opportunities and mitigate risks effectively."

He then guided his team through a series of case studies and examples to illustrate the practical application of financial modeling in real-world scenarios. From revenue forecasting and expense projections to cash flow analysis and investment valuation, each example showcased the transformative impact of financial models on decision-making and performance management.

"As we embrace financial modeling, it's important to foster collaboration and communication across departments and functions," Michael emphasized, his gaze sweeping across the room. "By leveraging data-driven insights, we can make informed decisions that drive sustainable growth and value creation for GlobalTech."

As the team absorbed the insights shared during the discussion, a sense of empowerment filled the room. They knew that by building robust financial models and committing to data-driven decision-making, they could unlock new opportunities for success and growth for GlobalTech.

With the discussion concluded, Michael and his team continued their journey of financial planning and analysis, armed with the knowledge and perspectives gained from the exploration of financial modeling principles. They were determined to apply their newfound understanding to predict future outcomes and drive strategic decision-making for GlobalTech in the years to come.

Michael's Reflections on the Importance of Adaptability

As the discussion on Financial Planning and Analysis (FP&A) drew to a close, Michael paused to reflect on the importance of adaptability in navigating the ever-changing landscape of finance and business. Understanding the need to embrace change and respond effectively to new challenges, he shared his insights with his team, emphasizing the critical role of adaptability in driving success for GlobalTech.

With the team gathered in the conference room, Michael took a moment to address them, his demeanor thoughtful and reflective.

"My friends," he began, his voice carrying the weight of experience, "as we conclude our discussion on financial planning and analysis, I want to take a moment to reflect on the importance of adaptability in our journey."

He spoke of the dynamic nature of the business world, where market trends shift, technologies evolve, and new opportunities emerge unexpectedly.

"Adaptability is not just about reacting to change," Michael explained, his words resonating with wisdom. "It's about embracing change as an opportunity for growth, innovation, and improvement."

He shared anecdotes from his own experiences, recounting moments where adaptability had been the key to overcoming challenges and seizing new opportunities for GlobalTech.

"In times of uncertainty, it's adaptability that allows us to thrive," Michael continued, his tone resolute. "It's our ability to pivot, to innovate, and to learn from our experiences that sets us apart and drives our success."

He encouraged his team to remain open-minded and flexible, to embrace change as a catalyst for growth rather than a barrier to progress.

"As we continue our journey, let us remember that adaptability is not just a skill, but a mindset," Michael concluded, his gaze meeting each member of the team with unwavering determination. "Let us embrace change with courage and resilience, knowing that it is through our ability to adapt that we will achieve greatness for GlobalTech."

As Michael's words lingered in the room, a sense of determination filled the air. The team understood that adaptability was not just a buzzword, but a guiding principle that would shape their approach to financial planning and analysis—and ultimately, their success in the ever-changing world of business.

With renewed resolve, they prepared to face the challenges ahead, confident in their ability to adapt, innovate, and thrive in the face of uncertainty.

13

Chapter 13: Leveraging Technology in Accounting

Implementing ERP Systems to Streamline Processes

In the era of digital transformation, Michael turned his attention towards leveraging technology in accounting, recognizing its pivotal role in streamlining processes and driving efficiency for GlobalTech. Understanding the transformative power of Enterprise Resource Planning (ERP) systems, he gathered his team to explore strategies for implementing these advanced technologies to enhance the company's financial management.

In the innovation hub of GlobalTech's headquarters, Michael convened his team once more, the air buzzing with anticipation as they prepared to delve into the realm of technology in accounting.

"Good morning, everyone," Michael greeted, his voice filled with enthusiasm. "Today, we're going to explore the strategic implications of implementing ERP systems for GlobalTech.

By leveraging technology to streamline our processes, we can drive efficiency and enhance our competitiveness in the marketplace."

He began by framing the discussion, explaining the concept of ERP systems and their importance in integrating financial, operational, and managerial processes. With clarity and precision, he outlined the key components of ERP implementation, including system selection, data migration, and user training.

"As we implement ERP systems, it's essential to adopt a holistic approach that considers the needs of our organization and aligns with our strategic objectives," Michael explained, his tone focused. "By leveraging ERP systems as strategic tools, we can optimize our processes, improve data accuracy, and make informed decisions that drive sustainable growth for GlobalTech."

He then guided his team through a series of case studies and examples to illustrate the practical application of ERP systems in real-world scenarios. From streamlining procurement and inventory management to automating financial reporting and analysis, each example showcased the transformative impact of ERP systems on organizational efficiency and effectiveness.

"As we embrace ERP systems, it's important to foster collaboration and communication across departments and functions," Michael emphasized, his gaze sweeping across the room. "By leveraging technology to streamline our processes, we can unlock new opportunities for innovation and drive excellence in everything we do."

As the team absorbed the insights shared during the discussion, a sense of excitement filled the room. They knew that by implementing ERP systems and committing to digital transformation, they could unlock new opportunities for efficiency and growth for GlobalTech.

With the discussion concluded, Michael and his team continued their journey of leveraging technology in accounting, armed with the knowledge and perspectives gained from the exploration of ERP implementation principles. They were determined to apply their newfound understanding to drive efficiency, enhance competitiveness, and achieve excellence for GlobalTech in the digital age.

The Role of Automation and Robotics in Accounting

As the discussion on leveraging technology in accounting continued, Michael shifted his focus towards exploring the transformative role of automation and robotics in driving efficiency and accuracy for GlobalTech. Understanding the potential of these advanced technologies to revolutionize traditional accounting processes, he gathered his team to delve into strategies for integrating automation and robotics into the company's financial management practices.

In the innovation lab of GlobalTech's headquarters, Michael convened his team once more, the atmosphere alive with anticipation as they prepared to explore the realm of automation and robotics in accounting.

"Good morning, everyone," Michael greeted, his voice filled with anticipation. "Today, we're going to explore the strategic implications of automation and robotics in accounting for GlobalTech. By harnessing the power of technology to automate repetitive tasks, we can drive efficiency and enhance accuracy in our financial processes."

He began by framing the discussion, explaining the concept of automation and robotics and their potential to streamline accounting workflows. With clarity and precision, he outlined the key components of automation and robotics implementation, including process analysis, technology selection, and integration with existing systems.

"As we embrace automation and robotics, it's essential to adopt a forward-thinking approach that leverages technology to enhance our capabilities," Michael explained, his tone focused. "By automating repetitive tasks, we can free up valuable time and resources to focus on strategic activities that drive value for GlobalTech."

He then guided his team through a series of case studies and examples to illustrate the practical application of automation and robotics in accounting. From invoice processing and expense management to financial reporting and compliance, each example showcased the transformative impact of these technologies on organizational efficiency and effectiveness.

"As we integrate automation and robotics into our accounting processes, it's important to foster a culture of innovation and continuous improvement," Michael emphasized, his gaze sweeping across the room. "By embracing technology as a strategic enabler, we can unlock new opportunities for efficiency, accuracy, and growth for GlobalTech."

As the team absorbed the insights shared during the discussion, a sense of excitement filled the room. They knew that by embracing automation and robotics and committing to digital transformation, they could revolutionize their accounting practices and position GlobalTech for success in the digital age.

With the discussion concluded, Michael and his team continued their journey of leveraging technology in accounting, armed with the knowledge and perspectives gained from the exploration of automation and robotics principles. They were determined to apply their newfound understanding to drive efficiency, enhance accuracy, and achieve excellence for GlobalTech in the era of digital transformation.

Utilizing Data Analytics for Deeper Financial Insights

As the exploration of technology in accounting progressed, Michael turned his attention towards the transformative power of data analytics in uncovering deeper financial insights for GlobalTech. Understanding the potential of data-driven decision-making to drive strategic growth, he gathered his team to delve into strategies for harnessing the power of data analytics to enhance the company's financial management practices.

In the data hub of GlobalTech's headquarters, Michael convened his team once more, the atmosphere buzzing with anticipation as they prepared to explore the realm of data analytics in accounting.

"Good morning, everyone," Michael greeted, his voice filled with enthusiasm. "Today, we're going to explore the strategic implications of utilizing data analytics for GlobalTech. By harnessing the power of data to uncover actionable insights, we can drive informed decision-making and enhance our competitiveness in the marketplace."

He began by framing the discussion, explaining the concept of data analytics and its potential to unlock valuable insights from financial data. With clarity and precision, he outlined the key components of data analytics implementation, including data collection, analysis, and visualization.

"As we embrace data analytics, it's essential to adopt a data-driven approach that leverages technology to extract meaningful insights from our financial data," Michael explained, his tone focused. "By harnessing the power of data analytics, we can gain a deeper understanding of our financial performance and identify opportunities for improvement and growth."

He then guided his team through a series of case studies and examples to illustrate the practical application of data analytics in accounting. From trend analysis and predictive modeling to risk assessment and fraud detection, each example showcased the transformative impact of data analytics on organizational decision-making and performance management.

"As we utilize data analytics, it's important to foster a culture of data literacy and continuous learning," Michael emphasized, his gaze sweeping across the room. "By empowering our teams with the tools and skills needed to leverage data effectively, we can unlock new opportunities for innovation and drive excellence in everything we do."

As the team absorbed the insights shared during the discussion, a sense of empowerment filled the room. They knew that by embracing data analytics and committing to data-driven decision-making, they could unlock new opportunities for success and growth for GlobalTech.

With the discussion concluded, Michael and his team continued their journey of leveraging technology in accounting, armed with the knowledge and perspectives gained from the exploration of data analytics principles. They were determined to apply their newfound understanding to drive informed decision-making and achieve excellence for GlobalTech in the data-driven age.

Embracing Cloud Computing for Real-Time Access

As the discussion on technology in accounting unfolded, Michael directed his attention towards the transformative potential of cloud computing in providing real-time access to financial data for GlobalTech. Understanding the importance of agility and accessibility in today's fast-paced business environment, he gathered his team to explore strategies for embracing cloud computing to enhance the company's financial management practices.

In the digital hub of GlobalTech's headquarters, Michael convened his team once more, the air charged with anticipation as they prepared to delve into the realm of cloud computing.

"Good morning, everyone," Michael greeted, his voice filled with anticipation. "Today, we're going to explore the strategic implications of embracing cloud computing for GlobalTech. By harnessing the power of the cloud to access financial data in real-time, we can drive agility and enhance our competitiveness in the marketplace."

He began by framing the discussion, explaining the concept of cloud computing and its potential to revolutionize how financial data is stored, accessed, and managed. With clarity and precision, he outlined the key components of cloud computing adoption, including data migration, security, and scalability.

"As we embrace cloud computing, it's essential to adopt a forward-thinking approach that leverages technology to enhance our capabilities," Michael explained, his tone focused. "By embracing the cloud, we can access financial data anytime, anywhere, and empower our teams to make informed decisions on the go."

He then guided his team through a series of case studies and examples to illustrate the practical application of cloud computing in accounting. From real-time reporting and collaboration to disaster recovery and scalability, each example showcased the transformative impact of cloud computing on organizational agility and efficiency.

"As we embrace cloud computing, it's important to prioritize data security and compliance," Michael emphasized, his gaze sweeping across the room. "By partnering with reputable cloud service providers and implementing robust security measures, we can ensure the integrity and confidentiality of our financial data."

As the team absorbed the insights shared during the discussion, a sense of excitement filled the room. They knew that by embracing cloud computing and committing to digital transformation, they could unlock new opportunities for efficiency, agility, and growth for GlobalTech.

With the discussion concluded, Michael and his team continued their journey of leveraging technology in accounting, armed with the knowledge and perspectives gained from the exploration of cloud computing principles. They were determined to apply their newfound understanding to drive innovation and achieve excellence for GlobalTech in the digital age.

Exploring Blockchain Applications in Accounting

As the discussion on technology in accounting progressed, Michael turned his attention towards exploring the innovative potential of blockchain technology in revolutionizing accounting practices for GlobalTech. Understanding the disruptive power of blockchain in ensuring transparency, security, and efficiency, he gathered his team to delve into strategies for exploring blockchain applications to enhance the company's financial management practices.

In the innovation lab of GlobalTech's headquarters, Michael convened his team once more, the atmosphere alive with anticipation as they prepared to explore the realm of blockchain technology.

"Good morning, everyone," Michael greeted, his voice filled with enthusiasm. "Today, we're going to explore the strategic implications of exploring blockchain applications in accounting for GlobalTech. By harnessing the power of blockchain to enhance transparency and security, we can drive efficiency and trust in our financial processes."

He began by framing the discussion, explaining the concept of blockchain technology and its potential to revolutionize how financial transactions are recorded, verified, and reported. With clarity and precision, he outlined the key components of blockchain adoption, including distributed ledger technology, smart contracts, and digital assets.

"As we explore blockchain applications, it's essential to adopt a forward-thinking approach that leverages technology to enhance our capabilities," Michael explained, his tone focused. "By embracing blockchain, we can improve the accuracy and integrity of our financial data and streamline our accounting processes."

He then guided his team through a series of case studies and examples to illustrate the practical application of blockchain in accounting. From audit trails and fraud detection to supply chain management and regulatory compliance, each example showcased the transformative impact of blockchain on organizational transparency and efficiency.

"As we explore blockchain applications, it's important to collaborate with industry partners and regulatory authorities to ensure alignment with best practices and standards," Michael emphasized, his gaze sweeping across the room. "By fostering collaboration and innovation, we can unlock new opportunities for efficiency, trust, and growth for GlobalTech."

As the team absorbed the insights shared during the discussion, a sense of excitement filled the room. They knew that by exploring blockchain applications and committing to digital transformation, they could revolutionize their accounting practices and position GlobalTech as a leader in the digital age.

With the discussion concluded, Michael and his team continued their journey of leveraging technology in accounting, armed with the knowledge and perspectives gained from the exploration of blockchain principles. They were determined to apply their newfound understanding to drive innovation and achieve excellence for GlobalTech in the blockchain era.

Ensuring Cybersecurity in Financial Management

As the discussion on technology in accounting neared its conclusion, Michael shifted the focus towards the critical importance of cybersecurity in safeguarding GlobalTech's financial management practices. Understanding the growing threats posed by cyberattacks and data breaches, he gathered his team to delve into strategies for ensuring robust cybersecurity measures to protect the company's financial assets and data integrity.

In the secure boardroom of GlobalTech's headquarters,

Michael convened his team once more, the atmosphere tinged with solemnity as they prepared to address the topic of cybersecurity.

"Good morning, everyone," Michael greeted, his voice tinged with gravity. "Today, we're going to explore the strategic implications of ensuring cybersecurity in financial management for GlobalTech. By prioritizing cybersecurity, we can protect our financial assets and data integrity from evolving cyber threats."

He began by framing the discussion, emphasizing the importance of cybersecurity in today's digital landscape and its critical role in mitigating risks and safeguarding financial information. With clarity and urgency, he outlined the key components of cybersecurity measures, including network security, data encryption, and employee training.

"As we ensure cybersecurity in financial management, it's essential to adopt a proactive approach that anticipates and addresses potential threats," Michael explained, his tone resolute. "By implementing robust cybersecurity measures, we can prevent unauthorized access to financial data and mitigate the risk of cyberattacks and data breaches."

He then guided his team through a series of case studies and examples to illustrate the potential consequences of cybersecurity vulnerabilities in financial management. From ransomware attacks and phishing scams to insider threats and malware infections, each example underscored the importance of vigilance and preparedness in safeguarding GlobalTech's financial assets.

"As we ensure cybersecurity, it's important to prioritize collaboration and information sharing among internal stakeholders and external partners," Michael emphasized, his gaze unwavering. "By fostering a culture of cybersecurity awareness and resilience, we can strengthen our defenses and protect GlobalTech from cyber threats."

As the team absorbed the insights shared during the discussion, a sense of urgency filled the room. They knew that by prioritizing cybersecurity and committing to proactive measures, they could protect GlobalTech's financial assets and data integrity from cyber threats.

With the discussion concluded, Michael and his team reaffirmed their commitment to ensuring cybersecurity in financial management, armed with the knowledge and perspectives gained from the exploration of cybersecurity principles. They were determined to apply their newfound understanding to safeguard GlobalTech's financial assets and uphold its reputation as a trusted leader in the digital age.

14

Chapter 14: Preparing for the Future

Understanding Sustainability Accounting

As GlobalTech charted its course towards the future, Michael recognized the importance of sustainability accounting in driving long-term success and responsible business practices. Understanding the growing emphasis on environmental and social responsibility, he gathered his team to delve into strategies for understanding sustainability accounting and its implications for the company's financial management practices.

In the conference room bathed in natural light at GlobalTech's headquarters, Michael convened his team once more, the atmosphere imbued with a sense of purpose as they prepared to explore the realm of sustainability accounting.

"Good morning, everyone," Michael greeted, his voice filled with determination. "Today, we're going to explore the strategic implications of understanding sustainability accounting for GlobalTech. By embracing sustainability accounting, we can integrate environmental, social, and governance factors into our financial management practices and drive long-term value creation."

He began by framing the discussion, explaining the concept of sustainability accounting and its significance in measuring and reporting the company's impact on the environment, society, and economy. With clarity and conviction, he outlined the key components of sustainability accounting, including carbon footprint analysis, social impact assessment, and stakeholder engagement.

"As we understand sustainability accounting, it's essential to adopt a holistic approach that considers the interconnectedness of environmental, social, and economic factors," Michael explained, his tone resolute. "By embracing sustainability accounting, we can enhance transparency, accountability, and resilience in our operations and create value for all stakeholders."

He then guided his team through a series of case studies and examples to illustrate the practical application of sustainability accounting in driving responsible business practices. From renewable energy investments and waste reduction initiatives to diversity and inclusion programs, each example showcased the transformative impact of sustainability accounting on organizational performance and reputation.

"As we embrace sustainability accounting, it's important to prioritize collaboration and dialogue with internal and external stakeholders," Michael emphasized, his gaze sweeping across the room. "By fostering a culture of sustainability and innovation, we can pave the way for a more sustainable future for GlobalTech and society as a whole."

As the team absorbed the insights shared during the discussion, a sense of purpose filled the room. They knew that by understanding sustainability accounting and committing to responsible business practices, they could drive positive change and create value for GlobalTech and its stakeholders.

With the discussion concluded, Michael and his team continued their journey of preparing for the future, armed with the knowledge and perspectives gained from the exploration of sustainability accounting principles. They were determined to apply their newfound understanding to drive sustainability and long-term success for GlobalTech in the years to come.

Implementing Integrated Reporting Practices

As GlobalTech embraced the future with a commitment to sustainability, Michael recognized the importance of implementing integrated reporting practices to effectively communicate the company's value creation story to stakeholders. Understanding the need for transparency and accountability in reporting, he gathered his team to delve into strategies for implementing integrated reporting practices and showcasing GlobalTech's holistic value proposition.

In the sleek boardroom of GlobalTech's headquarters, Michael convened his team once more, the atmosphere charged with anticipation as they prepared to explore the realm of integrated reporting.

"Good morning, everyone," Michael greeted, his voice filled with purpose. "Today, we're going to explore the strategic implications of implementing integrated reporting practices for GlobalTech. By embracing integrated reporting, we can communicate our financial performance, environmental impact, and social contributions in a cohesive and transparent manner."

He began by framing the discussion, explaining the concept of integrated reporting and its significance in providing a comprehensive view of the company's value creation process. With clarity and conviction, he outlined the key components of integrated reporting, including financial, environmental, social, and governance factors.

"As we implement integrated reporting practices, it's essential to adopt a holistic approach that reflects the interconnectedness of our business activities and their impact on society and the environment," Michael explained, his tone resolute. "By embracing integrated reporting, we can enhance transparency, accountability, and trust with our stakeholders and build a more sustainable future for GlobalTech."

He then guided his team through a series of case studies and examples to illustrate the practical application of integrated reporting in showcasing GlobalTech's holistic value proposition. From financial performance metrics and environmental stewardship initiatives to social impact programs and governance practices, each example showcased the transformative impact of integrated reporting on stakeholder engagement and perception.

"As we implement integrated reporting practices, it's important to prioritize collaboration and alignment across all functions and departments," Michael emphasized, his gaze sweeping across the room. "By fostering a culture of transparency and accountability, we can demonstrate our commitment to responsible business practices and create value for all stakeholders."

As the team absorbed the insights shared during the discussion, a sense of purpose filled the room. They knew that by implementing integrated reporting practices and embracing transparency, GlobalTech could effectively communicate its value creation story and inspire trust and confidence among stakeholders.

With the discussion concluded, Michael and his team continued their journey of preparing for the future, armed with the knowledge and perspectives gained from the exploration of integrated reporting principles. They were determined to apply their newfound understanding to drive sustainability and long-term success for GlobalTech in the years to come.

The Impact of AI and Machine Learning on Accounting

As GlobalTech continued its journey towards the future, Michael turned his attention towards the transformative impact of artificial intelligence (AI) and machine learning on accounting practices. Recognizing the potential of these advanced technologies to drive efficiency and innovation, he gathered his team to delve into strategies for understanding and harnessing the power of AI and machine learning in the company's financial management practices.

In the innovation lab of GlobalTech's headquarters, Michael convened his team once more, the atmosphere buzzing with excitement as they prepared to explore the realm of AI and machine learning.

"Good morning, everyone," Michael greeted, his voice filled with anticipation. "Today, we're going to explore the strategic implications of the impact of AI and machine learning on accounting for GlobalTech. By embracing these advanced technologies, we can drive efficiency, enhance accuracy, and unlock new opportunities for innovation in our financial management practices."

He began by framing the discussion, explaining the concepts of AI and machine learning and their potential to revolutionize how financial data is processed, analyzed, and reported. With clarity and precision, he outlined the key components of AI and machine learning adoption, including automation, predictive analytics, and pattern recognition.

"As we explore the impact of AI and machine learning on accounting, it's essential to adopt a forward-thinking approach that leverages technology to enhance our capabilities," Michael explained, his tone focused. "By embracing AI and machine learning, we can automate repetitive tasks, identify insights from large volumes of data, and make data-driven decisions to drive value for GlobalTech."

He then guided his team through a series of case studies and examples to illustrate the practical application of AI and machine learning in accounting. From automated invoice processing and fraud detection to predictive forecasting and financial analysis, each example showcased the transformative impact of these technologies on organizational efficiency and effectiveness.

"As we harness the power of AI and machine learning, it's important to prioritize collaboration and continuous learning among our teams," Michael emphasized, his gaze sweeping across the room. "By fostering a culture of innovation and experimentation, we can unlock the full potential of these technologies and position GlobalTech as a leader in the digital age."

As the team absorbed the insights shared during the discussion, a sense of excitement filled the room. They knew that by embracing AI and machine learning and committing to digital transformation, they could revolutionize their accounting practices and drive success for GlobalTech in the years to come.

With the discussion concluded, Michael and his team continued their journey of preparing for the future, armed with the knowledge and perspectives gained from the exploration of AI and machine learning principles. They were determined to apply their newfound understanding to drive innovation and achieve excellence for GlobalTech in the digital age.

Addressing Globalization and Its Effects on Accounting Practices

As GlobalTech adapted to the evolving landscape of globalization, Michael turned his attention towards understanding and addressing its effects on accounting practices. Recognizing the interconnectedness of global markets and the complexities it brings to financial management, he gathered his team to delve into strategies for navigating the challenges and opportunities presented by globalization.

In the strategy room overlooking the bustling cityscape from GlobalTech's headquarters, Michael convened his team once more, the atmosphere alive with anticipation as they prepared to explore the impact of globalization on accounting practices.

"Good morning, everyone," Michael greeted, his voice projecting authority. "Today, we're going to explore the strategic implications of addressing globalization and its effects on accounting for GlobalTech. By understanding and adapting to the complexities of global markets, we can ensure the relevance and effectiveness of our accounting practices in a rapidly changing world."

He began by framing the discussion, explaining the concept

of globalization and its implications for financial management, including cross-border transactions, currency fluctuations, and regulatory compliance. With clarity and insight, he outlined the key challenges and opportunities presented by globalization, including the need for harmonized accounting standards and the importance of cultural competence in financial reporting.

"As we address globalization, it's essential to adopt a global mindset and embrace diversity in our approach to accounting practices," Michael explained, his tone authoritative. "By understanding the unique challenges and opportunities presented by different regions and markets, we can tailor our accounting practices to meet the needs of a diverse and interconnected world."

He then guided his team through a series of case studies and examples to illustrate the practical implications of globalization on accounting practices. From navigating international tax laws and reporting requirements to managing foreign exchange risk and cultural differences in financial reporting, each example showcased the importance of agility and adaptability in addressing the effects of globalization.

"As we navigate the complexities of globalization, it's important to prioritize collaboration and knowledge sharing among our teams," Michael emphasized, his gaze sweeping across the room. "By leveraging our collective expertise and experience, we can develop innovative solutions and best practices to drive success for GlobalTech in a globalized world."

As the team absorbed the insights shared during the discussion, a sense of determination filled the room. They knew that by understanding and addressing the effects of globalization on accounting practices, they could position GlobalTech for success in the increasingly interconnected global marketplace.

With the discussion concluded, Michael and his team continued their journey of preparing for the future, armed with the knowledge and perspectives gained from the exploration of globalization's effects on accounting practices. They were determined to adapt and thrive in a rapidly changing world, ensuring GlobalTech remained at the forefront of financial excellence in the global arena.

Evolving Role of Management Accountants in a Digital Age

As GlobalTech embraced the digital age with fervor, Michael recognized the imperative to understand and adapt to the evolving role of management accountants in this transformative era. Acknowledging the convergence of technology and finance, he gathered his team to delve into strategies for navigating the changing landscape and maximizing the potential of management accountants in driving success for GlobalTech.

In the innovation hub of GlobalTech's headquarters, Michael convened his team once more, the atmosphere charged with anticipation as they prepared to explore the evolving role of management accountants in the digital age.

"Good morning, everyone," Michael greeted, his voice resonating with purpose. "Today, we're going to explore the strategic implications of the evolving role of management accountants in a digital age for GlobalTech. By understanding and embracing the opportunities presented by technology, we can empower our management accountants to drive innovation, efficiency, and strategic decision-making."

He began by framing the discussion, explaining the changing dynamics of the management accounting profession in response to advances in technology, data analytics, and automation. With insight and foresight, he outlined the key competencies and skills required for management accountants in the digital age, including proficiency in data analysis, strategic thinking, and technological literacy.

"As we navigate the evolving role of management accountants, it's essential to foster a culture of continuous learning and professional development," Michael explained, his tone decisive. "By investing in training and upskilling initiatives, we can equip our management accountants with the tools and knowledge they need to thrive in a rapidly changing environment."

He then guided his team through a series of case studies and examples to illustrate the practical implications of the evolving role of management accountants in the digital age. From leveraging data analytics to inform strategic decision-making to implementing automation to streamline financial processes, each example showcased the transformative impact of technology on the role of management accountants.

"As we embrace the digital age, it's important to prioritize collaboration and cross-functional teamwork," Michael emphasized, his gaze sweeping across the room. "By working closely with colleagues in IT, finance, and other departments, we can leverage technology to drive innovation and create value for GlobalTech."

As the team absorbed the insights shared during the discussion, a sense of optimism filled the room. They knew that by understanding and embracing the evolving role of management accountants in the digital age, they could position GlobalTech for success in an increasingly competitive marketplace.

With the discussion concluded, Michael and his team continued their journey of preparing for the future, armed with the knowledge and perspectives gained from the exploration of the evolving role of management accountants. They were determined to embrace technology, drive innovation, and achieve excellence for GlobalTech in the digital age and beyond.

Continuous Professional Development and Lifelong Learning

As GlobalTech embarked on its journey into the future, Michael emphasized the critical importance of continuous professional development and lifelong learning for the company's success in the digital age. Understanding the rapid pace of change and the need for agility in adapting to new technologies and industry trends, he gathered his team to delve into strategies for fostering a culture of learning and growth at GlobalTech.

In the learning center of GlobalTech's headquarters, Michael convened his team once more, the atmosphere charged with enthusiasm as they prepared to explore the importance of continuous professional development and lifelong learning.

"Good morning, everyone," Michael greeted, his voice brimming with energy. "Today, we're going to explore the strategic implications of continuous professional development and lifelong learning for GlobalTech. By investing in the growth and development of our employees, we can ensure that we remain agile, innovative, and competitive in the digital age."

He began by framing the discussion, explaining the importance of staying abreast of industry trends, technological advancements, and best practices in management accounting. With passion and conviction, he outlined the benefits of continuous professional development, including enhanced job satisfaction, increased productivity, and career advancement opportunities.

"As we prioritize continuous professional development, it's essential to create a supportive learning environment where employees feel empowered to explore new ideas and acquire new skills," Michael explained, his tone encouraging. "By investing in training programs, workshops, and mentorship initiatives, we can foster a culture of learning and growth that propels GlobalTech forward."

He then guided his team through a series of case studies and examples to illustrate the practical implications of continuous professional development and lifelong learning. From attending industry conferences and webinars to pursuing professional certifications and participating in peer learning networks, each example showcased the diverse opportunities available for employees to expand their knowledge and expertise.

"As we embrace continuous professional development, it's important to encourage a growth mindset and celebrate learning achievements," Michael emphasized, his gaze reflecting his belief in the power of education. "By recognizing and rewarding employees who invest in their professional development, we can create a culture where lifelong learning is valued and celebrated."

As the team absorbed the insights shared during the discussion, a sense of determination filled the room. They knew that by embracing continuous professional development and lifelong learning, they could unlock their full potential and contribute to the success of GlobalTech in the digital age.

With the discussion concluded, Michael and his team reaffirmed their commitment to personal and professional growth, armed with the knowledge and inspiration gained from the exploration of continuous professional development principles. They were determined to embrace learning as a lifelong journey and seize the opportunities that lay ahead for themselves and for GlobalTech.

15

Chapter 15: Conclusion: Mastering Financial Excellence

Michael's Reflections on His Journey and Growth

As Michael looked back on his journey of mastering financial excellence at GlobalTech, he felt a sense of pride and accomplishment. From the challenges he faced to the successes he achieved, his experiences had shaped him into a stronger, more resilient leader. Now, as he stood before his team to share his reflections, he knew that their collective efforts had propelled GlobalTech to new heights of financial excellence.

In the executive boardroom adorned with accolades and achievements, Michael gathered his team one final time, the atmosphere tinged with nostalgia as they prepared to conclude their journey together.

"Good morning, everyone," Michael began, his voice steady with emotion. "As we come to the end of our journey of mastering financial excellence, I wanted to take a moment to reflect on the incredible growth and transformation we've experienced together."

He spoke from the heart, recounting the challenges they had faced and the milestones they had reached. From the early days of uncertainty to the moments of triumph and celebration, each step had been a testament to their collective dedication and resilience.

"As I look back on our journey, I'm filled with gratitude for each and every one of you," Michael continued, his voice filled with sincerity. "Your hard work, dedication, and unwavering commitment to excellence have been the driving force behind our success."

He paused, allowing his words to sink in, before turning his attention to the future.

"As we move forward, let us carry with us the lessons we've learned and the bonds we've formed," Michael said, his gaze sweeping across the room. "Let us continue to strive for excellence in everything we do, knowing that together, there is no challenge we cannot overcome."

He concluded with a heartfelt expression of gratitude to his team, acknowledging their contributions and their shared journey towards financial excellence.

"To each and every one of you, thank you," Michael said, his voice filled with emotion. "It has been an honor and a privilege to lead this team, and I look forward to continuing our journey together, towards even greater heights of success."

As the team applauded, a sense of camaraderie and unity filled the room. They knew that their journey of mastering financial excellence was far from over, but with Michael's leadership and their collective determination, they were ready to face whatever challenges lay ahead.

CHAPTER 15: CONCLUSION: MASTERING FINANCIAL EXCELLENCE

With the conclusion of the chapter and the book, Michael and his team left the boardroom with a renewed sense of purpose and a commitment to continue their pursuit of financial excellence, knowing that their journey was just beginning.

The Transformation of the Company's Financial Health

As Michael stood in the boardroom, his eyes swept across the familiar faces of his colleagues and team members. The atmosphere was electric with anticipation. This was the moment they had all worked so hard for, the moment to reflect on the remarkable transformation of GlobalTech's financial health.

"Good afternoon, everyone," Michael began, his voice steady but filled with emotion. "Today, we celebrate not just the end of a journey, but the beginning of a new era for GlobalTech. An era marked by financial excellence and resilience."

He clicked the remote, and the screen behind him lit up with charts and graphs depicting the company's financial trajectory. The transformation was staggering. From the brink of financial instability to unprecedented profitability, the visual representation told a story of relentless effort, strategic innovation, and unwavering commitment.

"Just a few years ago, we were facing severe financial discrepancies and operational inefficiencies," Michael continued, the memories of countless late nights and intense strategy sessions flooding back. "But we didn't back down. We faced those challenges head-on, and look where we are now."

He highlighted the key initiatives that had driven their success. The implementation of advanced costing systems, the overhaul of the budgeting process, and the adoption of new technologies had all played crucial roles. Each step had been meticulously planned and executed, with the team working tirelessly to ensure every detail was accounted for.

"Our financial health is not just about numbers on a spreadsheet," Michael said, his tone passionate. "It's about the culture of excellence we've cultivated. It's about the strategic decisions we've made and the innovative solutions we've implemented. It's about the people in this room who have given their all to see GlobalTech thrive."

He turned to Sarah, his mentor, who had been a pillar of support and wisdom throughout their journey. "Sarah, I owe so much of our success to your guidance. You've taught me the importance of strategic thinking and the value of mentorship. Thank you for believing in us."

The team erupted in applause, a tangible expression of their appreciation for Sarah's contributions. She nodded graciously, her eyes shining with pride.

Michael continued, "We've seen tangible improvements in our cost reporting, streamlined our operations, and significantly enhanced our financial stability. Our EBITDA has increased by 25%, and our profit margins are the highest they've ever been. But beyond these metrics, we've built a foundation that will support our growth for years to come."

He paused, letting the magnitude of their achievements sink in. The room was silent, each person reflecting on their part in this incredible transformation.

"Looking ahead, we know that challenges will continue to arise," Michael said, his voice firm with resolve. "But I have no doubt that with the foundation we've built and the principles we've embraced, we will not only meet those challenges but turn them into opportunities for further growth and excellence."

As he wrapped up his presentation, Michael felt a profound sense of accomplishment and pride. The transformation of GlobalTech's financial health was a testament to their collective effort, strategic foresight, and unwavering dedication.

"Thank you all for your hard work, your resilience, and your commitment to excellence," Michael concluded. "Together, we have transformed GlobalTech into a beacon of financial excellence, and I look forward to continuing this journey with all of you."

With that, the room erupted in applause once more. The team members, buoyed by their shared success and the promise of a bright future, felt ready to take on whatever challenges lay ahead, confident in their ability to achieve continued financial excellence under Michael's steadfast leadership.

Key Takeaways for Aspiring Management Accountants

As the book on mastering financial excellence drew to a close, Michael recognized the importance of sharing key takeaways for aspiring management accountants. Understanding the value of imparting wisdom and guidance to the next generation of finance professionals, he gathered his thoughts to distill the most important lessons learned from his journey.

In the serene setting of his office, Michael reflected on the insights and experiences that had shaped his career. With a sense of purpose, he began to outline the key takeaways for aspiring management accountants, eager to inspire and empower them on their own paths to success.

"Dear readers," Michael began, his words flowing with

conviction, "as you embark on your journey in the field of management accounting, I offer you these key takeaways to guide and inspire you along the way."

He spoke from the heart, distilling his years of experience into actionable advice and timeless wisdom. From the importance of embracing change and innovation to the value of continuous learning and personal growth, each takeaway resonated with the aspiring management accountants who would read his words.

"As you navigate the complexities of the finance world, remember to stay curious, stay adaptable, and above all, stay true to yourself," Michael concluded, his voice filled with warmth and encouragement. "For it is through your passion, your perseverance, and your dedication to excellence that you will truly master financial excellence and make a lasting impact on the world."

With his message of inspiration and guidance conveyed, Michael felt a sense of fulfillment knowing that he had passed on his knowledge and insights to the next generation of finance professionals. As the book closed on this chapter of his journey, he looked forward to the future, confident that the aspiring management accountants who followed in his footsteps would carry on his legacy of financial excellence with pride and determination.

Future Trends and Challenges in Management Accounting

As Michael concluded his reflections on mastering financial excellence, he turned his attention to the future trends and challenges in management accounting. Understanding the importance of staying ahead of the curve and anticipating industry shifts, he gathered his team one final time to discuss the evolving landscape and the opportunities and obstacles it presented.

In the boardroom filled with anticipation, Michael addressed his team with a sense of urgency and purpose.

"As we bid farewell to this chapter of our journey, it's crucial that we look ahead to the future," Michael began, his voice resonating with authority. "The world of management accounting is constantly evolving, and it's our responsibility to stay informed and prepared for the challenges and opportunities that lie ahead."

He delved into the emerging trends shaping the field, from the increasing adoption of artificial intelligence and data analytics to the growing emphasis on sustainability and corporate social responsibility. With clarity and foresight, he outlined the potential impact of these trends on financial management practices and the role of management accountants in driving organizational success.

"However, with these opportunities come challenges," Michael continued, his tone grave yet determined. "From cybersecurity threats to regulatory complexities, the future of management accounting is fraught with obstacles that we must be prepared to overcome."

He encouraged his team to embrace innovation, adaptability,

and resilience in the face of these challenges, knowing that their collective strength and determination would see them through any adversity.

"As we embark on this journey into the future, let us do so with courage, conviction, and a commitment to excellence," Michael concluded, his words echoing in the boardroom. "For it is through our perseverance and determination that we will continue to master financial excellence and shape the future of management accounting for generations to come."

With a renewed sense of purpose and determination, Michael and his team left the boardroom, ready to face the future head-on and continue their pursuit of financial excellence in an ever-changing world.

Michael's New Role as a Mentor to Emerging Professionals

As Michael concluded his reflections on mastering financial excellence, he felt a newfound sense of responsibility to mentor emerging professionals in the field of management accounting. Recognizing the importance of paying it forward and sharing his knowledge and experience with the next generation, he embraced his new role with enthusiasm and determination.

In his office adorned with accolades and memories of past achievements, Michael contemplated the significance of mentoring emerging professionals.

"As I reflect on my journey, I realize that one of the most rewarding aspects of my career has been the opportunity to mentor and guide others," Michael mused, his thoughts drifting to the aspiring professionals who looked to him for inspiration and guidance.

CHAPTER 15: CONCLUSION: MASTERING FINANCIAL EXCELLENCE

With a sense of purpose, he resolved to dedicate himself to mentoring emerging professionals, eager to impart his wisdom and support their growth and development.

"Dear readers," Michael began, addressing the emerging professionals who would follow in his footsteps, "as you embark on your journey in the field of management accounting, know that you do not walk alone."

He shared his insights and advice, encouraging them to embrace challenges, seek opportunities for growth, and never lose sight of their potential to make a difference in the world.

"As your mentor, I am here to support you, guide you, and champion your success," Michael concluded, his voice filled with warmth and encouragement. "Together, let us continue to strive for excellence, inspire one another, and shape the future of management accounting for generations to come."

With a renewed sense of purpose and dedication, Michael embraced his new role as a mentor, knowing that by empowering emerging professionals, he could leave a lasting legacy of leadership and mentorship in the field of management accounting.

Final Thoughts on Achieving Financial Excellence through Management Accounting

As Michael prepared to conclude his reflections on mastering financial excellence, he knew that his final thoughts on achieving financial excellence through management accounting would leave a lasting impression on his team and readers alike. With a sense of reverence for the journey they had undertaken together, he gathered his thoughts to share his parting words of wisdom and inspiration.

In the quiet solitude of his office, Michael reflected on the profound impact that management accounting had on GlobalTech's success and the lessons he had learned along the way.

"As we come to the end of this journey, I am reminded of the transformative power of management accounting in driving financial excellence," Michael began, his voice imbued with a sense of gravitas. "Through strategic planning, innovation, and a commitment to excellence, we have demonstrated the profound impact that effective financial management can have on an organization's success."

He spoke from the heart, sharing his insights and reflections on the principles that had guided their journey to financial excellence. From embracing change and fostering a culture of continuous learning to leveraging technology and data-driven insights, each principle illuminated the path to success in management accounting.

"As we move forward, let us carry with us the lessons we have learned and the values that have guided us on this journey," Michael continued, his words resonating with his team and readers alike. "For it is through our unwavering commitment to excellence and our relentless pursuit of innovation that we will continue to achieve financial excellence and make a meaningful impact on the world."

He concluded with a message of gratitude and hope, thanking his team for their dedication and hard work and expressing his confidence in their ability to continue their journey towards financial excellence.

"As we close this chapter and embark on new adventures, let us never forget the transformative power of management accounting in shaping the future of organizations and in-

CHAPTER 15: CONCLUSION: MASTERING FINANCIAL EXCELLENCE

dustries," Michael said, his voice filled with reverence. "For together, we have proven that with passion, perseverance, and a commitment to excellence, anything is possible."

With his final thoughts shared, Michael felt a sense of closure and fulfillment knowing that their journey towards financial excellence had left a lasting legacy of leadership and innovation in the field of management accounting. As he closed the chapter on this part of his career, he looked forward to the future with optimism and excitement, knowing that the principles they had embraced would continue to guide them on their journey towards even greater heights of success.

About the Author

Goodson Mumba is a multifaceted individual known for his diverse expertise and prolific contributions across various fields. As an infopreneur, Management Consultant, thought leader, and spiritual leader, he has inspired countless individuals through his insightful teachings and impactful writings. Mumba is also an accomplished author, with several notable works to his name, including "Understanding Corporate Worship," "The Years I Spent in a Week," "Management By Harmony," "The CEO's Diary," "Change to Change" and "Creative Thinking for results" His literary works span topics ranging from business management to personal development and spirituality, reflecting his broad range of interests and insights.

With a Master of Business Leadership (MBL) and a Bachelor of Arts in Theology (BTh), Mumba brings a unique blend of business acumen and spiritual wisdom to his work. His educational background is further enriched by a Group Diploma in Management Studies, providing him with a solid foundation in organizational dynamics and leadership principles. Additionally, Mumba holds diplomas in Education Psychology, Leadership and Management Styles, Organizational Behaviour, Financial Accounting, Economic Growth and Development, and Project Management, showcasing his commitment to continuous learning and professional development.

Mumba's expertise extends beyond traditional academic disciplines, encompassing areas such as Neuro-Linguistic Programming (NLP) and Positive Psychology. His diverse skill set is complemented by a range of certifications, including Creative Problem Solving and Decision Making, Life Coaching Fundamentals and Techniques, Professional Life Coaching, and Performance Management System Design. These certifications reflect Mumba's dedication to equipping himself with the tools and knowledge necessary to empower others and drive positive change.

As an author, Mumba's writings reflect his deep understanding of human nature, organizational dynamics, and spiritual principles. His works offer practical insights, actionable strategies, and inspirational guidance for individuals seeking personal growth, professional success, and spiritual fulfillment. Mumba's holistic approach to life and leadership resonates with readers worldwide, making him a respected figure in both the business and spiritual communities.

Overall, Goodson Mumba's diverse background, extensive knowledge, and profound insights make him a sought-after speaker, mentor, and author. His commitment to excellence, lifelong learning, and service to others continues to inspire individuals to unlock their full potential and lead lives of purpose and significance.

Goodson Mumba is renowned for initiating the concept of Management by Harmony, revolutionizing traditional management practices with a focus on balanced and holistic approaches. He has authored two influential books on this subject: "Introduction to Management by Harmony" and its sequel, "Management by Harmony."

Mumba's work has significantly impacted the field, offering innovative strategies for fostering organizational harmony and efficiency. His contributions continue to shape contemporary management theories and practices.

www.ingramcontent.com/pod-product-compliance
Lightning Source LLC
Chambersburg PA
CBHW071827210526
45479CB00001B/33